"The world needs more leaders, and in Boss or Leader *Dave simply and cleverly facilitates the visualization process of your unique leadership style. This book is for YOU!"*

— **Elizabeth McCormick**,
International Motivational Leadership Speaker,
Former US Army Black Hawk Pilot

"Boss or Leader *gives business owners the power to radically enhance their companies. Ferguson has done a masterful job of creating a road map to organizational leadership."*

— **Judy Robinett**,
Bestselling Author,
How to Be a Power Connector and Crack the Funding Code

"Thought provoking and richly rewarding."

— **Ken Dunn**,
Author, *The Greatest Prospector in the World*

BOSS OR LEADER

BOSS OR LEADER

ARE YOU LEADING FOR A LIVING OR LIVING TO LEAD?

DAVE FERGUSON

NEXT CENTURY
PUBLISHING

Boss or Leader
Are You Leading for a Living or Living to Lead?
Expanded 2nd Edition

Published by Next Century Publishing
Las Vegas Nevada
www.NextCenturyPublishing.com

ISBN: 978-1-68102-159-1
Library of Congress Control Number: 2016938343

Printed in the United States of America

Contents

BOSS OR LEADER

INTRODUCTION

What exactly is leadership?

My good friend and mentor, John C. Maxwell says, "Leadership is influence, nothing more, nothing less." Do you agree?

Peter Drucker defines leadership like this: "The only definition of a leader is someone who has followers." Do you agree?

Bill Gates says this about leadership: "As we look ahead into the next century, leaders will be those who empower others." Do you agree?

Warren Bennis defines it like this: "Leadership is the capacity to translate vision into reality." Do you agree?

Dwight Eisenhower said this about leadership: "Leadership is the art of getting someone else to do something you want done because he wants to do it." Do you agree?

It seems that everyone has his or her own definition of leadership, so who is right? Since you are reading this introduction, you have the desire to learn more about leadership. The question now becomes: With most everyone taking a different view on defining leadership, how do *you* define it? Reading and studying this book will serve as a good start to helping you find your own definition. I also highly recommend finding a mentor to help guide you along the way.

I think we make leadership much more difficult than it needs to be. I believe that the above quotes are all correct, but none of them have fully defined the art of leadership. My experience tells me we all define leadership differently, based on our unique style and personality.

I'm a simple guy and I like to keep things pretty simple when I write. You will find this book, simply put, is one that can help shape your leadership style, inspire people to follow you for more than a paycheck, and increase your ability to develop other leaders.

Before you read further, I want to be clear on something: there is a difference between being a *leader* and being a *boss*. I don't believe there is such thing as a natural born leader. Leaders are educated and developed. A boss, on the other hand, is merely a title given to someone in charge. In fact, the word boss may invoke images of someone demanding compliance, someone who is bossy and only wants his or her own way. My hope is that this exploration of the differences between bosses and leaders will add value to your life and help you to turn your employees into followers.

Are you ready? Then read, learn and enjoy!

Regards,

Dave Ferguson

CHAPTER 1

———— ✤ ————

The Power Of Perseverance

*"Perseverance is the hard work you do after you get
tired of doing the hard work you already did."*

~ Newt Gingrich

When it comes to the topic of leadership, I don't think there is a better place to start than the topic of perseverance. I discovered at an early age that if you want to become successful in life, if you want to be a true leader, then the ability to persevere is of utmost importance.

Have you ever set a goal you knew would not be easy to reach, would require effort, continuous commitment, even doing something you have never done before? I have, and most of the time it took a lot more work than I had originally planned. The one word to describe what it means to reach the mark—*perseverance*.

We identify something that we want, figure out a path to get there, and start the process. When the going gets tough, we take another look at the goal and decide that maybe it's not worth the struggle to achieve it. As a professional coach, I have heard this story time and time again over the last seven years. I'd like to point out the difference between a leader and a boss. A leader will decide to push forward and lead by example. A boss, however, will push *you* forward. He or she is not willing to do the work and demands that you do it.

I suppose it's been both a blessing and a curse, but when I was about ten years old I realized that the only one who was going to create a successful path for Dave was Dave. Maybe it was the circumstances I faced growing up. Maybe it is just the fact that I won't settle for less than I desire. The fact remains, when I put my mind to something, I achieve it. As a leader, I choose a path of perseverance. And that is what true leaders do—they make a conscious decision to achieve, which in turn shows those under their leadership how to persevere in their own lives.

Writing this book is a great example. It is something I have wanted to do for quite some time, but as is usually the case, there are obstacles—time, resources, self-limiting beliefs, and more. But there was just a part of me that knew this needed to get done. I needed a way to share my story of accomplishment. Why? Because that's what I do. I help those who are willing to invest in themselves achieve the things that are important to them, even when they are not easy to attain.

After spending the past twenty-five years in the financial world and seven years in professional coaching, I have seen one constant over time. If you want to succeed, you need to be driven, you need to be focused, and you need to persevere.

Many of the clients with whom I work struggle with the concept of perseverance. Many believe being consistent or persistent will produce the results they are looking for. But herein lies the problem: being consistent and persistent, although important along the pathway to success, does not always produce results. Perseverance adds the one ingredient that makes the difference. Perseverance is what gets you through those roadblocks and obstacles. And perseverance is a character trait that leaders need to cultivate and demonstrate.

*****

As an athlete, I love learning from and being inspired by others. Here is a great story on perseverance:

PAINFUL BUT POSSIBLE: A STORY OF PERSEVERANCE

I did not want to go running.

I definitely did not want run eight or ten miles.

This planned run was training for a half-marathon (13.1 miles) I hoped to complete in three weeks. I had already done a few long runs ranging from eight to twelve miles, so I didn't really need to do this run.

For some past races, I hadn't trained as well as I should have, so back in January, I had been realistic but ambitious, as I put together my training plan and I'd scheduled numerous long runs.

Now I wondered why.

Ambition

Each of us has ambitions—feats we dream of accomplishing in various areas of our lives.

It's easy to begin these ventures with high energy and great plans, but we often struggle with commitment and follow-through.

Too often we don't set goal, or if we do, they are unrealistic. Then when life doesn't happen as we planned, our energy for the venture fades.

That's why we need a healthy balance of proper goals and perseverance to see us through. For me, running has been a tangible teacher of both.

Running through the pain

Running has been part of my life since I took my first cautious steps about two decades ago, after having three sons in less than five years. Running not only became my exercise, it also brought balance to my body, mind and spirit.

The perseverance that running requires carried over into other areas of life: from owning a business to tending flower gardens to parenting (who knew those adorable babies would take so much perseverance?).

One day, I woke up in a hospital bed to discover that twelve days prior I had almost died and nearly lost my leg in an accident. My doctors weren't sure if I would ever walk again. Talk about needing perseverance.

I replayed memories of tough runs during my recovery, especially when doing thousands of toe curls, knee bends and leg lifts in physical therapy.

I don't remember my first steps at age two, but I'll never forget my first steps at age thirty-eight. My doctors and therapists cheered with me, but told me that running was a thing of my past. I tried to accept that, but my decade of running had taught me that our bodies are stronger than we realize.

I figured that as long as I "did what I could, where I was, with what I had," as Theodore Roosevelt had said, who knew how far my body could recover?

Perseverance

I walked regularly. I did stretches. I walked some more. Each step I took gave me strength and energy to take more steps the next time.

Perseverance paid off.

Four years post-accident, I had a new doctor who didn't think I was crazy to consider running again; instead, he encouraged me. I tried it, cautiously. It was painful, but possible. Exhausting, but exhilarating.

Step by step, my body grew stronger until I was a runner again.

Finishing well

So on that recent dreary Monday when I wanted to bail on a run, I didn't. Completing well at the upcoming half-marathon was important to me, so I would follow the necessary plan to do that. The run was not glamorous. There was no "high." It was one determined step after another.

As my friend and I slowly checked off the miles (we did nine), I replayed the endless hours of therapy I had done, reminding myself that I had pushed through with that, so I could push through with this run. As I did that, I was struck by the realization that perseverance creates more perseverance.

So as you dream of new ventures to accomplish, do some research, plan and prepare, set realistic goals. Review the goals. And then, persevere.

Because not only will your current venture benefit from the perseverance, but your next big venture will also benefit from it.[1]

*****

Let's be honest; anything worth doing is going to come with challenges and some of these challenges are going to seem insurmountable. So what are you going to do? Look for another plan that will eliminate them? That might work, but eventually you will end up right back where you started. At some point, you'll start the same circle over again, producing frustration and anxiety, until you decide to persevere and overcome those challenges.

As I reflect on my experience in the corporate world, I can tell you there is a clear difference between the way a boss and a leader approach a challenge. A boss manages things and scales their productivity according to many things they can get done and how many items they can check off their list. Leaders, on the other hand, lead people, and evaluate their performance by how well their followers perform. That performance will get the same things done that the boss accomplished, but with one very large difference—the focus on *getting* the things done centers on what is *being* done. The focus on who is doing the work is more about the culture of the business and not the product or service.

During discussions with clients, I have found it interesting how much I've learned from just the words spoken. Bosses talk about the employees. Leaders talk about their people. Bosses are on the management team. Leaders are on the leadership team. Some of you may think this is no more than using different words to say the same thing. I challenge you to ask your "employees" what they think. Are you valuing your people or only the work they are doing? There is a big difference!

The generally accepted thought has been that if you work harder and faster, you will get more done. This may not be an inaccurate statement, but is this sustainable? Will this train of thought really produce the results that you are looking for?

Perseverance is not something that shows up on a job description. Perseverance is something that comes from within. It's not something you can teach, but it is something you can learn. Perseverance is the act of doing something because you believe in the vision of what will be produced by your effort. This is where the difference between success and failure is found. When we believe in something, when we feel like we matter, when we feel we are part of a bigger cause, then we will persevere. Making a difference is what drives us.

How do we get our employees to become followers? How do we get them to move from doing what they *have* to do to doing what they *want* to do?

The first thing is to realize that a boss won't be able to accomplish this. Followers need a leader. I heard it once said that people don't buy into what you do; they buy into why you do it.

Think about that a minute.

Followers follow a person, not a list. *If you want followers, you need to be a leader.* Far too many times, I have had "bosses" ask me why their employees won't follow them. Why they do not appear to be engaged. Why they do not seem to take pride in their work. My favorite response to these questions is, "Why should they?" There is not enough room in this book to list the responses I have received when asking this question. Some of the most common: "It's their job," or, "That's what they are paid to do." Do you see anything wrong with this picture?

The simple truth is that a strong team is willing to persevere through the tough times, the obstacles and the roadblocks—as long as the team has a strong leader. John Maxwell says, "Everything rises and falls on leadership." I believe he is spot on. If there is no leadership, there will be no vertical movement.

If you want followers, be a leader others can follow. Give them ownership or what they are doing. Allow them to be part of the decision making process. That doesn't mean they will necessarily be making the decisions. It does mean that you are willing to acknowledge they have a voice and their opinion matters. At the end of the day, people have both the desire and the need to feel valued. When you value your people—something that leaders know how to do—they will be willing to go the extra mile for you. They will want to follow you because they trust you.

Yes, I said it. Trust! Consider this: have you ever heard someone badmouth their boss? I already know your answer. Now let me ask you another question: How often have you heard someone badmouth their leader? When you started reading this book, you probably had some thoughts on whether or you are a boss or a leader. I am curious to know if your answer to that question has changed.

As we continue exploring the differences between a boss and a leader, I would suggest that in some areas you lead well, and in some areas you are simply a boss. Your ability to persevere will be important as you continue along your journey to becoming the leader you desire to be. The difference between success and significance will come from the perseverance demonstrated by those who follow you.

Are you a BOSS or a LEADER?

A BOSS believes her opinion is the most important because they are in charge. A LEADER thinks everyone's opinion matters because they are all integral members of the team, and perseverance comes from team unity and a shared mission.

A BOSS believes he or she needs to control everything and only gives out information he thinks is important. A LEADER wants the entire team to share in the process so the team will persevere, knowing they will share ownership in the success.

A BOSS believes the culture is something that is defined. A LEADER knows the culture is created through both celebrating success and persevering through adversity.

CHAPTER 2

———❖———

Clearing Up Your Vision

*"Positional leaders ignore the fact that every
person has hopes, dreams, desires, and goals of his
own. And leaders must bring their vision and the
aspirations of the people they lead together in a way
that benefits everyone."*

~ John C. Maxwell

I love it when a client brings up the topic of vision.
Any level of achievement is going to start with vision.
It amazes me how so many people struggle with this
concept. Most believe it is simply what you see for the
future and all you have to do is create a plan to bring
that vision into reality. In simple terms that is correct;
however, there are a few pieces of the "vision puzzle" that
are often left out of the equation.

In the business arena, vision will include many people
and, most likely, contain additional factors that will move
an organization toward fulfillment of that vision. The

failures that occur are the result of not allowing the vision to be flexible and to adapt as needed. Let me explain. We cast a vision that represents where we want to go in the future. We develop a plan to get there. Then what often happens is an obstacle, roadblock or challenge pops up along the way and we fail to make the proper course correction to deal with it.

Here is a major difference between those who achieve their vision and those who don't. There is an understanding, or lack thereof, that vision is not a destination, it is a journey. I have seen more than one successful business cast a vision, then move forward and try to navigate around each obstacle, instead of taking them on one-by-one along the way. This is a recipe for failure. Vision is *never* a destination; it is only a stopping point at the furthest location you can see at any given time.

Think about hiking in the mountains. Your vision can only take you to the next high point. You can't see beyond that. But once you get there, you have a full view in all directions, allowing you to extend the vision in order to keep going. If you approach one of those peaks as the final destination, you will remain stuck there and inevitably die a lonely death. It's no different in business or, for that matter, in your personal life. Each hilltop is only a stopping point along the way, and if you don't prepare to keep going, there you will remain.

This is what I have commonly seen in the business world. Many of my clients had become stuck on a mountain peak because they viewed their vision as a destination. Do you have a boss who rarely, or maybe never, lets you see beyond that next high point? Maybe he is not even providing the direction in which you are supposed to be headed. Bosses can be like that. The sad thing is, oftentimes they are not sharing the full vision because they do not know it themselves. Their vision and direction is such that you simply need to get to do what you're told, because that is where their current ends.

*****

Not everyone understands what a vision is or why it needs to be communicated, so here is a great example:

WHAT IS A VISION?

A vision is your big picture of the way things ought to be. It is your billboard image of what you are working toward.

For example, you may have a picture of all the different ways you want your neighborhood to be better. You may want a neighborhood that has clean streets.

You may want people to watch out for each other so that crime is less likely to take place. You may want a neighborhood in which people know each other well enough to be able to solve problems together.

Everyday, as you go about your life, you may find yourself thinking about all the ways things could be better. If you put together all the pieces of how things should be, you have an overall vision.

Your overall vision is like a billboard. It is a picture of your ideal [of what you want to see become a reality] that gets your ideas across powerfully, accurately, and quickly.

Once you have a vision, you tell people about it and use it to lead people.

WHY DO YOU NEED TO COMMUNICATE YOUR VISION TO OTHERS?

Why communicate your vision to others? Because no one can decide to follow you until they know what direction you're headed in.

If your vision is one that strikes a chord with many people and if you can communicate it well, people will join you in reaching towards your goals.

Sharing a vision is a central role of a leader—a vision gives people a bigger picture of what things can be like. It helps people raise their hopes and expectations; it inspires them. When people are inspired, they are more likely to work on something.[1]

*****

Travel is a large part of my business and every trip includes a vision that will bring me back home. But getting back home is not the end of the vision. Every trip is part of a bigger vision, a vision for me to make a larger impact with my clients, as well as in my personal journey. I have big aspirations to work on a broader scale both with my client base and geographically. What I have learned about vision over the years has allowed me to understand this: to see my vision become my reality, I need to be intentional. And, every action I take is part of a greater vision. Once I realized that my vision quest was a journey and not a destination, I was able to navigate the challenges with much more intention and success.

I love what John Maxwell says about navigation: "Anyone can steer a ship, but it takes a leader to chart the course." The same principle applies to vision. A boss can cast a vision, but it takes a leader to see the destination as merely a stopping point along the way. Bosses rarely see beyond the next peak. Leaders are already planning ahead before they arrive at their current peak. The trail could be washed out, the map outdated, but a leader will keep moving, adjusting and readjusting toward that vision with intentional actions that will eventually empower them to reach their ultimate goal.

When it comes to vision, one of the biggest difference between bosses and leaders is who they take with them along the way. Bosses will usually cast the vision and say, "Go." Leaders will cast the vision and say, "Let's go!" Vision is not an individual activity. Casting a vision requires you cast it *with* others not *to* others. Even if the vision is created by one individual, when cast effectively, it will include others within the game plan to achieve it.

Have you ever had someone say to you, "Here is the vision I have for you"? Maybe it was worded as, "Here is my vision for the future." How much more impact would there have been had it been cast as "our vision"? Vision is not a road traveled alone, yet bosses take that drive every day, only to wonder why they are disappointed with their final destination.

Leaders, on the other hand, are willing to sit on the same bus and participate in the conversation with their team, while sharing their vision. Fulfilling a vision takes team effort; the stronger your team, the more likely you will reach your goal. While a boss tries frantically to re-route around traffic and construction, the leader uses those challenging times to grow his people, allowing them to be part of the solution rather than just passengers along for the ride.

Vision is something that needs to be cast such in a way that everyone can participate. If you want others to share in your vision, make them part of it. Allow them to have a say regarding the route you will travel; give them an opportunity to help navigate the tough times. If you want the most out of your people, give them ownership in the process and allow them to share in the wins, as well as feel the losses. These are the times that can build unity, create a culture that can withstand the storms and overcome adversity that occurs during any effort to succeed.

*****

The following is a continuation of the story I started earlier on page 11:

WHEN DO YOU NEED TO COMMUNICATE YOUR VISION?

All the time. Whenever you talk to people about your group or organization, tell people what you are working towards. The more you do it, the better you will get at it, and the more people will be willing to support you.

Even before you have formed a group or organization, it is important to talk about your vision. As you communicate it to others, you are creating a community of people who know about your idea and who potentially will support you.

HOW DO YOU CREATE A VISION?

Dreaming is the first step. Go ahead and dare to dream about what you can do and what is possible to accomplish. Don't be afraid to dream big. You can always scale down to meet the realities of the situation, but dreaming big allows you to think about ideas that may not seem likely, yet are in fact possible. Thinking big also forces you to think about the long term, always a useful thing to do.

Can you recall a time when you got a wild idea in your head and your heart started beating fast and you wondered what it would be like if you could make that idea happen?

Maybe you intermittently think, "Oh, that's impossible. How can I be so foolish as to think that!" However, often the ideas that feel foolish may have the most potential. They are often ideas that are new to the world. Learn to value and trust your hunches. If you get an idea that makes your heart sing, chances are good that others will come to sing along with you.

CLARIFY YOUR VISION

Once you have lots of ideas down on paper you have a good start. Now, sift through everything you wrote down and pick out what is most important to you. (Don't throw away the details, though; they are important for later, when you are communicating your vision.) Now, are there some general statements that express your most important ideas? Are there some powerful or compelling phrases or words that get to the heart of what you care about?

GET FEEDBACK ON YOUR VISION

Talk to people about your vision as much as you can. Tell them what you are thinking. Give them your big picture of things. Then listen. See if other people are concerned about the same things you are concerned about. See if people are interested in your picture of how things could be.

The more you talk to people and listen to them, the clearer your vision will become. First of all, you will get some practice speaking. Whenever a person talks, they have a chance to hear their thoughts out loud; as they listen to themselves, they get clearer on what they are trying to say.

Secondly, after listening to people respond to your ideas, your vision will probably change somewhat. You may want to incorporate some of their thinking into your own. Other people's ideas will help you make your vision stronger.

After talking to people about your vision for a period of time, you will get an idea of how strong your vision is. You will have a sense of whether other people get excited when you speak. Everyone doesn't necessarily have to agree with your vision for it to be a good one—but if people get animated and interested in talking with you about your vision, that is a sign that you are onto something.

DEVELOP AND COMMUNICATE THE DETAILS

After you test and reshape your big-picture vision, you should develop the details. You need to give people some specifics as to what your big picture will mean on a day-to-day level. You also have to tell people what steps you will take to get there, i.e., develop a plan. People may think your big picture is a meaningless mirage if you don't give them some ideas as to how you think things will actually change.

You don't have to have all the answers, but you need to have some ideas. If you have a vision of your neighborhood as one in which people from different cultural and racial backgrounds work together to prevent crime, what has to happen to get there? Do you need different church groups to set up a task force first? Do you need to set up some cultural sharing events? Do you, at some point, need to build a neighborhood group that can challenge city hall to provide better police protection for your neighborhood?

Write up some tentative ideas for how to get things done. The better your plan for reaching your vision, the more likely people will take you seriously and be willing to follow your lead.

Once you have confidence that your vision is sound, begin to put it out there as a way to gather support for your leadership and what you and your organization want to accomplish. Use your vision as a way to inspire people to act.

HELP PEOPLE TAKE OWNERSHIP OF A VISION

As a leader, you have to help people take your vision and make it their own. This is an important step in bringing people together to work toward a common goal. Members of a group need to have a shared vision and a sense of ownership in order to be committed to the group. That is key in helping people stay with a group for the long haul.

People don't need to agree with all the details of your vision in order to follow your lead. They will have different ideas about how to put a vision to use. That is fine and healthy. But in order to work together, people need to share an overall vision and some basic goals.

To help people take your vision and make it their own, you need to talk and listen. You shouldn't talk too much. You should mostly listen to peoples' thinking. If you really sit back and listen to people, they will tell you what is most important to them.

It may take people a long time to get to the point of telling you what is really important to them. They may have to tell you first about their children or a crummy experience they had with a politician. However, if you can listen long enough, people will tell you their thinking about how things should change.

A BALANCING ACT

At times people may not be ready to hear your vision of how things can be. Some people may disagree. Some may have so much of their attention taken by surviving day-to-day that it is difficult for them to listen to how things can be better. Also, people sometimes feel mistrustful, hopeless, discouraged, and cynical. Some people depend on a narrow picture of the world in order to feel secure.

Communicating a vision to people through that obstacle course can be tough. You often have to meet people where they are in order to establish some trust. As we talked about earlier, listening is an important tool in doing that.

But you also have to communicate the parts of your vision that people can relate to. They may not be ready to think about an overall plan for transforming your neighborhood. However, they may be able to think about doing something about the potholes in the streets. If so, talk about potholes. Talk to people "where they're at." Speak to their conditions and their personal needs. This will help you build some trusting relationships. Later you can do more.

On the other hand, it is sometimes important to say things that people are not quite ready to hear. People need to think about new ideas over a period of time before they can make sense of them. New ideas are important to introduce, even if they engender initial resistance. Often the strongest and most important ideas meet with resistance.

A leader has to lead. And the most important aspect of leadership is winning over the thinking of people to a vision of what things can be like.

SUMMARY

As you lead, you should be communicating your vision all the time. People look to leaders to inspire them and keep them on the right track. The more you are enthusiastic and clear about where you are going, the more likely it will be that people follow your lead.

Don't underestimate the power of your ideas and words. You, as much as anyone, have what it takes to lead others and to help them envision a better [way of doing business].[2]

*****

As a leader, here is the hard part of casting vision. We have discussed how you bring your people along the way and make them participants, not just spectators. But at the end of the day, you are the one responsible for the success, or the failure, of the journey. One of the most difficult challenges to deal with when moving from boss to leader is accepting responsibility for *everything* that happens. Bosses are quick to accept praise when things go right but look anywhere other than in the mirror when something goes wrong. Leaders share the praise. They also own up to the losses, while holding their teams accountable without public embarrassment.

If you want followers, you need to get your people engaged and willing to follow you. The only way that is going to happen is when they trust you. I will spend an entire chapter on the topic of trust but it needs to be part of the vision discussion as well. We need others, or followers, if we are going to see our vision come to life. The only way we get followers is by building trust, by acting such in a way that our followers will know they are safe taking the journey with us. Even when we empower them by incorporating them into the decision process, they need to know it is the leader who will eventually accept the responsibility of the outcome. Followers need to know we have their back, they are safe traveling with us. Leaders share the wins and own the losses.

Few of us want to go on a trip without knowing where we are headed. Many of my cross-country trips include connecting flights. If I am flying to Los Angeles I recognize that Atlanta may simply be a stop along the way, but I know that Los Angeles is where I am really going to end up. How would you feel if you were told you were going to Atlanta but when you arrived you discovered it wasn't your actual destination? This is the way bosses navigate the journey. They only provide part of the itinerary and then expect you to focus on the destination without even knowing what it is. Leaders provide the entire map to the best of their knowledge. They provide a vision that will allow others to participate during the entire trip.

Are you a BOSS or a LEADER?

A BOSS believes he or she is responsible to cast their vision and people should follow that vision. A LEADER believes in sharing their vision and acknowledges they can't accomplish it without the active support of his followers.

A BOSS believes they alone are responsible for any changes in direction related to the vision. A LEADER welcomes input from followers and course corrections involve feedback from the entire team.

A BOSS casts the vision and assumes followers will follow. A LEADER shares the vision and makes sure all of his or her followers understand it clearly so everyone is on the same page.

A BOSS creates a vision about what he or she knows and expects others to be involved. A LEADER makes sure followers are included in the vision so they can take ownership in the outcome.

CHAPTER 3

———— ❖ ————

Time For An Attitude Adjustment

*"Your attitude, not your aptitude,
will determine your altitude."*

- Zig Ziglar

You are not going to hear any groundbreaking information about attitude in this chapter because it has already been said. The problem is nobody wants to *listen*. We continue to tell other people they need an attitude adjustment when we are unwilling to change. Have you considered that you, yourself, might be part of the problem? If everyone around you has a bad attitude, maybe it's a reflection of your own behavior. Attitudes are contagious. Ask yourself what you may be spreading around the circles in which you run. And yes, this goes well beyond the workplace!

Simply put, your attitude is going to impact every aspect of your life; personal and professional will both be influenced one by the other, negatively or positively. We all know what a bad attitude produces—more bad attitudes. The real question is what caused the attitude to begin with. I recently read a statement that had me stop and think, even more than I usually do when I hear something that catches my attention: *We get what we create and what we allow.*

Hmm.

Think about that a minute.

What are you creating and what are you allowing in your life?

This is going to be a new piece of my coaching whenever attitude is part of the discussion. The more I think about this, the more I think this one little concept can do much more than simply change our attitude. I look back at the "attitude issues" I have dealt with over the years, including my own, and I can honestly say, in almost every situation, the negative attitudes were a result of allowing something external to control the actions. In other words, we have allowed someone else to control our behavior. Do you see the problem here?

I'll come back to this in a moment, but let's visit "control" for a moment. Control seems to be a topic that comes up often with both bosses and leaders and, in most instances, is something we don't want to give up. I almost find that amusing because poor attitudes are often, in fact most times, exactly that, giving up control. This may be hard for some to grasp because we pride ourselves on staying in control. Yet the minute something goes other than the way we want, the blood pressure goes up and those around run for cover.

I have watched this scenario play out over and over again. Bosses continue to ask what they can do to improve the attitudes of their people, when they are unwilling to change themselves. Funny how so many people are anxious to change their condition or their circumstance but are unwilling to change themselves. I find humor in those who give up control yet hold onto the belief that someone or something is responsible for their attitude. The bottom line is that *no one is responsible for your attitude but you.*

You bosses out there probably love that last statement. I can hear you right now: "That's right, they are responsible for their attitudes. So what's it going to take for them to improve?" If that was your thought, then stop it! Bosses and leaders both have responsibilities to the bottom line but there is a big difference. I will explore this later but taking responsibility is integral to developing the right attitudes. Bosses feel responsible *for* their people and their success; leaders feel responsible *to* their people and providing them the opportunity to succeed. Did you notice who holds the control in the previous statement?

Let's explore why we see different attitudes from those being managed by bosses and those being led by leaders.

A boss wants to control; therefore, he is most likely going to look to control the conditions or circumstances around the people over whom he is in charge. He wants it done his way and holds to the belief that it is his job to control the environment in which his people are performing. Is this the type of environment you currently find yourself in? Remember, I said that people are responsible for their own attitudes and our environment generally has a lot to do with our attitude. If someone else is controlling our environment, our control is somewhat limited. Keep in mind that we are looking at the difference between bosses and leaders. Regardless of the circumstance, you are still responsible for your own actions.

Here is my point: as a boss or a leader, it is our responsibility to (1.) create an environment conducive to a positive attitude; (2.) allow our people to focus on the task at hand instead of spending all their energy overcoming adversity, while trying to maintain a positive attitude in a hostile environment. Bosses struggle with this concept. They set their people up for failure by creating an environment that is going to stand in the way of a positive atmosphere.

Leaders, on the other hand, set up their followers for success. Leaders create an environment that provides their followers with the opportunity to make their own decisions and maintain a positive attitude. Why? Because they have been allowed to stay in control of the conditions in which they are working. For example, a follower may have been working at his desk all morning and just wants to get up and take walk to clear his head and get the blood flowing again. No problem, right? Not until the boss jumps in his face and asks him why he thinks he can just go for a stroll when everyone else is hard at it. A leader will see something like this and make a suggestion that everyone take a break when needed with no threat of questioning their work habits.

That may be an oversimplified example, but do you see the difference in thinking and how each of the scenarios may illicit a much different response when it comes to attitude? Control is a huge issue with all of us, not just the Type A people who want to make sure that everything gets done, gets done correctly and gets done on time. Control, or loss of it, is one of the biggest reasons people feel stress. I have found that one of the biggest contributing factors to a poor attitude is a high stress level or a stressful environment.

Environment is another theme or topic that you will often see throughout this book. By default, we tend to become a product of our environment, good or bad. Our attitude is one of the first things that follows suit when it comes to the environment in which we are working. Bosses worry about what their workspace, or environment, will produce. Leaders know that creating the right environment—one that will create less stress and produce more positive attitudes—will deliver the desired results with much less effort.

Leaders accept responsibility for their people and the environment they are creating, while providing a workplace conducive to positive attitudes. Allowing their followers the latitude to control their own schedule, and sometimes their workplace itself, will not only empower them but also build up these people in the process. Being in control of yourself and the environment in which you are working builds confidence. Confidence provides a greater desire to stay in control. Being in control reduces stress and less stress results in a more positive attitude.

I stated at the beginning of the chapter that I was not going to tell you anything you have not heard before. Hopefully, the way this chapter has been presented will change the way you look at your people. As a boss or leader, I suggest you look in the mirror first, if you feel your team's overall attitude could use some adjusting. Just as everything rises and falls on leadership, the attitude of your team will rise and fall on yours. Bosses will continue to hold their people responsible for a negative culture, while leaders will recognize any issues and infuse the team with positive thoughts, leading by example in order to achieve the desired results. Set your followers up for success and allow them to create an environment in which they can thrive. Have you ever seen anyone thriving with a bad attitude? Have you ever seen anyone with a bad attitude thrive? Just sayin'!

Are you a BOSS or a LEADER?

A BOSS focuses on what it will take for their followers to improve their attitude. A LEADER focuses on improving heir own attitude so as to lead by example.

A BOSS focuses on how he or she can more effectively control the work environment. A LEADER focuses on how they can give more control back to their followers so they can control themselves.

A BOSS tries to fill his environment with people with good attitudes. A LEADER creates an environment that will reduce stress and create a positive culture.

CHAPTER 4

———— ❦ ————

The Inspiration Equation

"In life you need either inspiration or desperation."

~ Tony Robbins

I believe one of the most misused words in life and business is motivation. Many look at motivation as a means to get others to do what they want them to do. Guess what? They are right. Motivation is a way to get others to do what you want them to do. But consider how much more productive your team would be, if they were doing not what *you* wanted them to do, but doing what *they* wanted to do!

The word you really want to think about is inspiration. There is a big difference between motivation and inspiration. I can't tell you how many times I have been working with a client and am asked, "How do I motivate my people?" My first response is to ask what the individual feels they are currently doing to motivate their people toward greater productivity. Most of the responses I receive are of the extrinsic nature. In other words, motivating by some type of compensation such as an increase in salary, bonus or an addition or increase in some other type of benefit such as vacation time, company vehicle, or better office location.

These extrinsic benefits will motivate in the short term but rarely sustain over time. Not all of my clients have missed the boat on this one. Many understand that inspiration is a much more beneficial approach to employee engagement, retention and overall increased performance. Can you guess what's coming next? Bosses motivate, leaders inspire.

I recognize there are several bosses out there who are motivating and getting results. I also recognize there are leaders who inspire and are getting better results, results that last longer over time. As I look back on my career in the financial world, it is obvious to me that the difference between motivation and inspiration is greater than many people might think. The problem is that many bosses have simply accepted that "achieving the numbers," is good enough. Our culture has become so driven by the numbers that we have started looking at employees as resources instead of people.

When you think about it, people are both our greatest asset and our greatest liability. When we look at people as a resource, we simply judge the productivity that the resource is producing. When the resource no longer produces what we expect, we just get rid of it and get another one. There have been numerous studies completed estimating the cost of employee turnover. The actual numbers vary depending on the industry, but the overall answer is clear: it costs a tremendous amount of money to train new employees. So we try to motivate existing employees by giving them a better return on their investment of time but we offer little investment in them as people.

*****

As a speaker and executive coach, I'm always looking for great material on leadership and business development. Forbes Magazine recently posted this article on how to inspire others:

3 SIMPLE, POWERFUL THINGS LEADERS CAN DO TO INSPIRE PEOPLE TO DO GREAT THINGS

Lately I've been thinking about the simple things leaders do, or fail to do, that have profound impact on their employees' perception of them, and on their employees' commitment and productivity.

Then recently I was speaking with someone who mentioned how a leader in her organization had recently lost a lot of credibility with his folks. When I got curious, she explained the situation: he had told them last fall that if they worked really hard to get a new product deliverable by a certain date, it would be reflected in their bonuses. They did, and it wasn't. Now he's going through the same thing with the 2.0 version of the same product, and his folks are (understandably) much less willing to go above and beyond the call of duty.

And today I got a press release about an interesting study conducted by Keas, a company that focuses on employee health and wellness. They interviewed over 100 HR professionals in the US on a variety of topics, most of them health and wellness-related. However, the finding that caught my eye (given my recent thinking about what CEOs can do differently), was this question: "In your experience, what are the top three Human Resources mistakes that every CEO makes?" And the top-scoring three responses:

64% – CEOs don't recognize what truly motivates employees.

41% – CEOs fail to lead by example in key HR initiatives.

32% – CEOs don't make company culture a priority.

I think these HR people are exactly right. Because all three of these actions (or non-actions) send a loud, clear message to employees: you are not that important to me.

THE 7 DEADLY SINS OF MANAGEMENT

That may sound brutal but they are true. Let me offer a couple of examples. This first one is about the dangers of not recognizing what motivates (or demotivates) employees. Earlier this week a client mentioned that when they moved into a new building recently, employee parking, which had been free in the old building, was going to be about $100/month per person in the new building. The CEO wanted to make everyone pay–he didn't think it would be a big deal for people. The man I was speaking to, his COO, convinced him that it would be hugely demotivating–that for someone making $30-40,000 a year, $1,200 a year for parking was definitely going to be a big deal. He also pointed out that the overall cost was going to be a wash; the rent in the new building was actually cheaper because parking wasn't included. He finally convinced the CEO that any savings realized would pale in comparison to the ill-will that would be generated by suddenly springing this added financial burden on his employees, and they decided to subsidize the parking fee, at least for the first year. Because $100/month was barely worth mentioning to the CEO, given his income, he thoughtlessly assumed it wouldn't matter to his employees. A great example of not understanding what's important and motivating to employees.

Here's another example, this one about the negative impact of not making company culture a priority. I've watched with sadness, over the past few years, as many of the best people have left one of our client companies. I believe it's primarily because the CEO refuses to recognize that she has allowed (and in some cases even encouraged) a very toxic workplace culture. Her people are overworked and under-communicated with; they feel pretty continually afraid of being yelled at, frozen out, or fired; they're asked to work long hours without being acknowledged; they don't have the tools or training they need to do their work well. Not surprisingly, performance and profitability are suffering. The CEO and board think the problems can be addressed by cutting costs, putting a few new people in key roles and finding new revenue streams: I think they're doomed to failure.

In both instances, the CEOs actions clearly carry that core message of "you're not that important to me, employees." And there's a simple equation attached to that: if a leader's people feel that they're not that important to him or her, then guess what–that leader, and the company, and the company's success are not going to be that important to them.

So what's a leader to do? Very simply: start by doing the three things those smart HR people in the Keas survey are saying you don't do.

Recognize what motivates your people. Get curious. Ask. And be willing to hear things that differ from what's motivating to you, or from what you think ought to be motivating to them. Talk to your HR people, if they're good and you respect them (and if they aren't and you don't…why are they working for you?) about what's most meaningful to people, and how you can incorporate that into your reward systems.

Support key HR initiatives by example, not just talk. Model the things you expect from others. Period. Here's what happens when you don't do this: Let's say you've just put in place a new performance management system, and you introduce it with great enthusiasm–but then never review your own direct reports, or promote and reward them based on your own whims, rather than according to the criteria you've established for the rest of the organization. You're communicating: 1) this may be good enough for you people–but I get to live by different rules, and 2) this (and you) are just not that important to me.

Create a strong, positive company culture. Start by finding out what your current culture is. There are lots of good employee survey mechanisms out there you can use to get a sense of what's going on. Then really take in the information–don't deny, avoid, or dismiss it. Sit down with trusted advisors and decide a handful of key things you can start doing, stop doing, or do differently as an organization to begin to address the biggest problem areas.

If you consistently do these three things as a leader, people will feel they matter to you, and they're much more likely to support you in achieving great business results. AND–big bonus–in tough times, they'll be there to help you and the company make it through.[3]

*****

As you read through this book you will find a common theme regarding your investment in people. I believe, and have witnessed, the greatest results come from investing in the person first. The resulting performance will simply be a bi-product of how great your investment is. Motivation will typically get them going but inspiration will keep them going and growing! If you want your people to produce more, you need to help them become more.

Here is the bottom line. Motivating through compensation does not meet the core need of most individuals. Work is a means to paying bills and putting food on the table. We all know we have to work, but also recognize we want more from what we do in order to be truly inspired. One of my colleagues was "motivated" for thirty years in the construction industry to a point where he did not even know what inspired him anymore. The motivation that provided a nice pay check, retirement program, company vehicle and other benefits left him with a major void in his life. He eventually left the industry to re-create his lost identity. Our identity is what inspires us. It's not about what we do. It's about who we are.

Bosses are concerned about what we do. Doing more with less has become the norm. Life becomes driven by meeting deadlines and sales quotas. I used to believe this philosophy until I realized I was simply trading time for dollars. There is more to life than a nice car, a big house and a fat savings account. Once I understood that I was only getting better at what I did, and really no better at who I was, the motivation didn't really work anymore. Can you see this in any of your followers, co-workers or employees? Leaders realize that by inspiring their people, business goals and developing a stronger team can be accomplished at the same time.

This was part of the reason that I left the corporate world to become a professional coach. I came to the realization that motivation would only take me so far, whereas inspiration would be the thing that separated success from significance. I knew the secret, and I wanted to share it with those who were willing to change from an extrinsically motivated business model to an intrinsic inspirational model. Much of my success, and the successes of my clients, has come from this shift in thinking. Motivation is on the outside; inspiration comes from within. Our own core belief system and that of our people is what will drive us to new and greater levels of achievement.

I know what you are thinking: *So how do I inspire the people I have been trying to motivate?* The answer will make all the difference in the world. Let's explore what I have seen happen when bosses who motivate become leaders who inspire. If you want to see results right away, then you are going to have to be authentic and transparent. If these words make you uncomfortable, then you are probably a boss. To inspire others, you need to show them you are willing to share in the struggle, to lead the way, even when it's difficult. You need to own the outcome of the decisions you make and be willing to admit when you are wrong.

These types of leadership behavior choices represent your commitment to a greater cause. People want to be working toward a bigger cause. They want to matter and be part of something greater than what they can achieve on their own. I won't suggest you can't motivate a large group but typically motivation is an individual thing. We are going to be motivated in different ways and will perform at different levels. Inspiration is bigger than that. Inspiration is about sustaining change that comes from within. External forces may influence inspiration but they can't kill it. Think about the greatest stories of achievement you have heard. Which word is typically used to describe the story—motivation or inspiration?

If you want to be a boss and motivate for results, offer some more money, another week of vacation time, a few more three day weekends or one of my favorites—a new job title. Do you really think any of these will produce consistent results over time? *Be a leader and inspire.* Show your people how they can become better at what they do *and* who they are. Start protecting your assets instead of limiting your liabilities. Focus on what can be done, not on what cannot.

If you really want to inspire others, wear your "why" on your shirt sleeve and let others know why you do what you do and why you want them to be part of it. Leaders will inspire their followers to perform, not because they have to but because they want to. Motivation suggests: in order to get something, I have to do something. Inspiration suggests: in order to do something, I need to become something. When we become more we will achieve more. Becoming more eliminates the need to be motivated. We are inspired by our own growth.

The great thing about inspiration is that it can sustain itself because it builds momentum along the way. Motivation needs to be continually refueled and when the fuel runs out, so does achieving the results. I have actually observed motivation as an addiction. Those who become accustomed to being motivated toward results stop performing when the motivation runs out. Leaders who inspire others see something different. Those they inspire start to inspire others. That's the momentum I am talking about.

Are you a BOSS or a LEADER?

A BOSS motivates others to do what they are required to do. A LEADER inspires others to do what needs to be done because they want to.

A BOSS makes sure his or her followers know what they need to do. A LEADER makes sure their followers know why it needs to be done.

A BOSS focuses on ways to get everything done. A LEADER focuses on making sure everyone has an opportunity to do everything they can.

CHAPTER 5

———✦———

Finding A Purpose That Matters

*"Knowing your purpose can dramatically enhance
your experience of life. Purpose-driven people
experience more fulfillment, more success, and
often greater financial rewards than other people.
Paradoxically, people who set out to live their
purpose often make more money than people who set
out to make money."*

~ Timothy Kelly

Purpose is one of the most important yet most difficult topics to understand. When asking the question, "What is your purpose?" I usually receive a response related to a person's job description. I struggled with this myself for quite some time and have come to this conclusion: The reason so many people get hung up on this topic is because it is being asked the wrong way. The question should not be, "What is your purpose?" But, "How are you serving your purpose?" Do you see the difference?

Asking the question, "What is your purpose?" suggests the person is just another piece of the puzzle, another resource that either functions or does not. Treat your people like a resource and they will act like one. You may be wondering why I feel that purpose is so important when it comes to leadership. It is fairly simple. Our purpose is what drives us, what fuels our human spirit to act, and what helps us to feel satisfied in what we have accomplished. Do you think any of this might be important to those following you?

Have you ever been told what to do and had no idea why you needed to be doing it? How did that make you feel? I struggle to understand how some bosses think their followers will do what they are told to do simply because, "'I said so." The boss replies, "They are not paid to think, they are paid to perform. I will do the thinking, that's what I am paid for." Really? I have actually heard that before. Bosses want people to serve a purpose—their purpose. Leaders know that to be effective, their followers need to be serving their own purpose.

I believe we have all been created to serve a unique purpose. That doesn't mean you can't do other things, but if you really want to feel fulfilled, then you need to be working within your purpose. It is interesting to see how much more productive employees are when they are working in a position they feel serves their purpose. Here is a little secret for you. The job your followers are in may have nothing to do with their purpose, but a leader can show how working that job can benefit their purpose indirectly. If you want to see a shift in the performance of your people, show them how they benefit from what they are doing. Doing something that serves one's purpose, directly or indirectly, will increase engagement and productivity every time.

This idea of serving one's purpose is huge. I don't want you to miss the point here. In both my corporate career and my career as a coach, the greatest productivity I have seen is when someone is living out their purpose through what they do. Some of you might be tempted to say that once someone becomes successful, they are obviously living out their purpose. I won't suggest that it can't happen this way, but my experience is that people simply perform at a higher level when they know what they are doing makes a difference and, most significantly, when that difference makes an impact in their own life.

Don't misunderstand me. No boss or leader will be able to create a job description that can serve the purpose of each of their followers. There is one big difference that separates bosses and leaders, however. Leaders show the *benefit* of being part of a team and communicate the purpose of the team. We all desire to be important, to make a difference, to create a legacy worth living. When we see we are part of the greater good and how our efforts impact others, it's easy to connect the dots to our individual purpose.

There needs to be a "why" in everything we do. Yet bosses fail to identify the why. There is not an individual out there who will move toward reaching their potential without a strong why. I heard a discussion recently and loved the comment that followed. The discussion was related to the intelligence of people and how that equated to performance. The comment: Key people don't necessarily need a high IQ, they need a high WhyQ. How cool is that?

I have also come to another conclusion about the way bosses think. Bosses think that a purpose can be created. They talk about growing the business and increasing profit margins. I get it. While these are important objectives and necessary for sustaining a business, will they sustain the followers? Leaders, however, take it a step further and show the benefit of strong growth and profitability. They paint a clear picture of where the growth and profits will lead, reaching more customers or clients, more job opportunities, better working conditions, more stable employment. These are all part of the bigger picture, a picture that matters. That is serving one's purpose.

How does a leader create an environment that allows for his followers to live their purpose? He starts by examining his own purpose. There are many tasks a leader needs to complete. One of the most important is to provide his followers with opportunities. It doesn't matter what we are doing, the belief that there is something more out there, just waiting for us, is one of the most inspiring gifts we can give our people. Think about it. I'm sure you've heard someone, when speaking of his current job, say things like, "I am in a dead-end job." or "I am going nowhere."

Serving our purpose is organic and alive. When there is no opportunity to serve our purpose, we feel empty and lost. Is that how you want your followers to feel? If that's how they feel, do you really think they will perform at a high level? Opportunities energize us, give us a reason to go on, a direction to travel. I am a firm believer there are no dead-end jobs, only dead-end bosses. Every business was designed for sustainability. Sustainability requires change. No longer are we able to exist, either in our personal or professional lives, by simply standing still and playing it safe. Opportunities are what allow us to remain in our purpose and find fulfillment in life.

Purpose can be a little tricky, and even leaders can mess this up. I know because I've seen it. The biggest mistake leaders make is thinking that a great opportunity will inspire others to action. Sometimes both leaders and bosses will create opportunities that don't match up with a purpose. The way to avoid this is by communicating with your people. Allowing your followers to be involved in creating opportunities is the best way to create opportunities that will be fulfilling.

Consider that it is very unlikely your followers are going to suggest an opportunity they would not want to be involved in. When leaders share their vision, identify the purpose of the business, then collaborate with their people on opportunities to grow the business or help it become more profitable, they find out the most interesting information. Remember, people want to be part of something bigger than what they can accomplish alone. They want to be part of the solution. The best way to create the future is to let your people create theirs. If you want to see your business grow exponentially, allow your people to create ways they can serve their purpose and yours. Do you think that people want to follow someone who allows them to create their own future? I sure do!

The first thing to do if you want to create a tribe of followers that will produce for you, and for the business, is to discover the best way for them to live out their purpose. Bosses are afraid the purpose of their people might not serve the business. Leaders know that without serving their purpose, their followers will never fully reach their potential, and neither will the business.

Are you a BOSS or a LEADER?

A BOSS focuses on the purpose of the business.
A LEADER focuses on the purpose of his or her people.

A BOSS looks for opportunities to make the business more efficient and profitable. A LEADER looks for opportunities for their followers to become more efficient, then watches the business become more profitable in the process.

A BOSS tries to create an environment and find the people who will fit into it. A LEADER seeks input from their followers and allows them to create their own future.

CHAPTER 6

───◆───

Never Compromise Your Character

"Be more concerned with your character than your reputation, because your character is what you really are, while your reputation is merely what others think you are."

~ John Wooden

No book can be written on leadership without addressing the topic of character. Can you think of someone whom you consider a strong leader but is *not* a person of character?

We are faced with decisions every day that put our character to the test, and some are subject to immediate review by the people with whom we work or live. These are the easy ones to deal with because all eyes are upon us. We are going to be judged immediately by our actions and, in most cases, we will take the easy way out by making a choice acceptable to the majority. These decisions usually come down to using the skills we have developed over time. We make the logical choice, the one most people would choose, then go on with our life. They account for only about ten percent of the decisions we make. Leaders and bosses will usually make similar choices under these circumstances.

So what about the other ninety percent? These decisions speak volumes about your leadership character. Most are made behind closed doors. Do you see the problem? You may have heard the saying that true character is what you do when nobody else is looking. I happen to believe this is a pretty accurate statement. Earlier in the book, I mentioned authenticity and transparency as being two traits that separate bosses and leaders. It just so happens that these words have a lot to do with character as well.

Character is not something for which you take classes or practice to get better. Character is who you are both when others are looking and when they aren't. It is who you are on the inside. Who you are on the inside should be who you are on the outside. This is called being congruent with yourself. I have met many bosses who had no understanding of this concept. You may know some. They are the ones you don't trust; those who put themselves in front of others; the ones who seem to have more excuses than solutions; the bosses who find fault in everyone or everything else. You know them.

I used to believe character was simply the act of making good decisions that were in the best interest of the whole. It didn't take long for me to understand that bosses can make those very same decisions. These are decisions based on leadership skills. In other words, they can be learned. Becoming a person of stronger character really comes down to your core belief system or your core values. This is what character is all about. Your core values are going to tell you what the right decision is to make. I know, we don't always do what we know is right; but the fact that we know something is wrong at least suggests we have some core values to depend on, when faced with difficult decisions.

Character is definitely a challenging topic to deal with. Of all the aspects of leadership, this is the one impacted by things not necessarily verbally communicated or written on paper. Character is really a combination of all the different ways we are influenced in our lives. I call this our "worldview." For example, children brought up in a culture of strong character are much more likely to be strong in character when they grow up. People working for a company with high moral and ethical values are more likely to make decisions in alignment with those values.

*****

HERE ARE TEN CHARACTER TRAITS THAT LEADERS SHOULD LIVE BY

1. Be Honest.

2. Demonstrate integrity.

3. Keep promises.

4. Be loyal.

5. Be conscientious.

6. Pursue excellence.

7. Be kind and caring.

8. Esteem all people.

9. Be fair.

10. Be a good citizen.

*****

I used to believe that people were just the way they were. Some were strong in character, some were not. But after dealing with issues of character for several years now, I have an entirely new understanding of character.

I still adhere to the premise that we don't learn character but we can be trained in it. As I mentioned earlier, our character is a combination of the influence that comes from our surroundings, our experiences and even other people. This is where leaders shine and bosses fail miserably. I suggest that both the environment we create and the culture we provide play a big role in the character of your business as well as the individuals in it. I believe that character is a product of both, and as you'll remember we have already discussed many differences between bosses and leaders, when speaking of environment and culture. Bosses work as part of an environment and typically continue working within the culture as it existed when they arrived. Leaders create both and in creating something new, something better, they also create a better workforce.

Another challenge is there are many key elements which play into character. Trust, respect and commitment are all subjects I will explore more deeply as we move along, and they are integral parts of character. It has been said that every failure in leadership comes down to a failure in character. I must agree. It only takes one mistake in character to ruin a business, a relationship or a reputation. *Character is huge*. It sets the tone for your team, your business and yourself.

Character can save you or take you down. It has that much power. If you want to be a person of strong character, let me suggest a few things. First, surround yourself with people whom you believe are of strong character. We become a product of those with whom we hang out.

Remember, bad company corrupts good character. I have heard many speakers say that we become the product of the five people with whom we spend the most time. Take a moment and think this through. With whom are you spending your time?

If you struggle to find the type of people you need in your life, then start reading about them. There is power in the books we read. We may not know the authors personally, but their stories can serve as an example on how to behave and how to set a better example for those around us.

Now let's take a look at how we can build a team of followers who will demonstrate the same levels of character we want for ourselves. It starts with you. You set the standard for what is acceptable and what is not. Regardless of what the policy is, your people will look to you to demonstrate the way to act and the process for making decisions. Don't expect them to perform at a higher level than you are providing. Take the time to explain why you are making the decisions you make or acting the way you are acting. *Confusion is a character killer.* Nothing will compromise your ability to lead faster than acting in a way that does not make sense, especially when you are not following the rules.

I have seen many successful and many struggling businesses over the years. One thing has been constant: those lacking character are not going to make it. Unity and cooperation inspire a team through the difficult times. Unity comes from trusting each other, respecting each other and staying committed to the greater cause. When you have a breakdown in character, you have a breakdown in the structure that holds the organization together.

One final thought. When you are strong in character, the "Why did they do that?" card is rarely played. People trust character, and leaders who have character can simply lead. Bosses, on the other hand, spend far too much time trying to justify the decisions they make because nobody understands their reasons or methods. Be true to yourself and true to your team, and people will follow you. Those who lack character will never have a large following.

Are you a BOSS or a LEADER?

A BOSS works on the 10 percent of leadership everyone can see—their skills. A LEADER works on the 90 percent that isn't seen, their character.

A BOSS expects their people to be trustworthy, respectful and committed. A LEADER behaves in a way that builds trust, shows respect and demonstrates commitment.

A BOSS only shares the decisions that worked out well. A LEADER shares most decisions and explains why they were made.

CHAPTER 7

———✣———

Making Failure Your Friend

"Far better to dare mighty things, to win glorious triumphs, even though checkered by failure…than to rank with those poor spirits who neither enjoy nor suffer much, because they live in a gray twilight that knows not victory nor defeat."

~ *Theodore Roosevelt*

One of the easiest ways to differentiate between bosses and leaders is how they deal with failure. Very few of us grew up believing that failure was a pathway to success, let alone an acceptable outcome. Today's thought leaders have made it a point to include their stories of failure and the lessons they've learned, which have become integral to their success. It has also become somewhat of a Catch-22. Our culture has become more receptive to the idea of failure because it can serve as a catalyst to success. We have also accepted failure as part of business in general, reducing the accountability bosses are willing to accept.

When failure occurs, bosses describe it as just part of business, then try and mitigate the fallout. Leaders, on the other hand, don't just accept failure; they embrace it and try to learn everything possible. Bosses look at failure as an example of what not to do again. Leaders look at failure as way to learn how to do things right. How can you tell if you are working with a boss or a leader? Simple—are they focusing on the problem or the solution? Bosses bring deficit-based thinking to the picture and work to avoid anything that may bring harm their way. Leaders will utilize asset-based thinking and seek to find the resources that can turn failure into success. *The key to dealing with failure is to learn from it, not lose from it.*

*****

I read a great article on learning from failure that I'd like to share it with you:

THE FOUNDATION FOR SUCCESS IS LEARNING FROM OUR FAILURES.

Each day we are provided with list of things we can do to be successful as entrepreneurs. We are given examples of very successful entrepreneurs who exemplify these traits. Then why is it that most people who embark on an entrepreneurial path don't succeed?

We ignore how we learn as humans. Our greatest lessons come from our mistakes and failures. In fact, if someone says he or she is a very successful entrepreneur and has never failed, you know they are lying.

Related: Afraid of Failure? Think Like a *Scientist* and Get Over It.

Having trained many entrepreneurs, I know the key for those who succeed is their ability to honestly appraise themselves. They reflect on the outcomes of their decisions and act with discipline to correct errors. One of the measures of entrepreneurial success is when a business is still around after four years. Here are some facts on startups:

- 25 percent fail in the first year.
- 36 percent have failed after the second year.
- 44 percent have failed after the third year.

The most common reasons for these failures are incompetence of the owner, going into business for the wrong reason and lack of clear focus. Note that rarely do startups fail because there is too little capital available. So what can you learn from this?

1. If you are going to start a business, get clear about the skills needed to run a successful company in that field. After the financial crisis of 2008, there was a flood of people starting new businesses because they lost their jobs. One of the common misunderstandings I hear is, "How hard could it be to run a business anyway?" It's not necessarily hard, it's just not what you think.

2. Now, make a clear assessment of your level of competence in the areas needed for success. This is critical. You shouldn't trust just your own perspective. Get three or more advisors who are successful business people and ask them to evaluate you. It may be uncomfortable but it may save your new business.

3. Determine what areas you are going to work on to improve your competence and in what areas you are going to find someone else to provide the expertise. You don't have to have all the answers. Maybe you are great in sales but not good at accounting. Then you need to make sure you hire an accountant who gives you strong feedback and accepts accountability for this area.

4. Develop a monthly practice of reconciliation of your business. Lay out your assumptions at the beginning of the month for sales, marketing, products, people and finance. When the month is over, see what you accomplished and

the lessons learned. Then incorporate this learning into the assumptions for next month.

The road to success isn't hard. It requires discipline and honesty. If you rigorously practice these simple steps, your chance of success with a new business will be greatly enhanced.[4]

*****

One of the biggest problems with failure has nothing to do with the outcome. Failure gets in our heads and breaks us down. Be honest: when you fail, don't you try and keep it from becoming headline news? Don't feel bad; no one likes to fail, which is why we are so quick to cover up. This is another easy way to tell the difference between bosses and leaders. You will only find out when a boss failed if there is no way to hide it. Even then, look for him to find someone or something to blame. Leaders are going to be the first to admit their failures, then bring in their followers with the intent of learning together so everyone can move forward.

Perseverance definitely helped me overcome failure while growing up and when I entered the business world. However, I look back on some of those experiences and realize I missed some opportunities to learn. I had a strong will and I was determined to succeed, regardless of the challenges I faced. That determination has helped me overcome many obstacles in my life. However, only recently have I truly been able to embrace failure so that I can learn from it. With each lesson learned, I have gained a better understanding of why failure is necessary for success.

With every failure comes a lesson, which is exactly what we need to eliminate the obstacles that can prevent us from finding success. Thomas Edison learned 20,000 ways *not* to build the light bulb. Do you think it was worth it? Here is the point: historically, we have run from failure because we did not get the expected results. Knowledge does not exist in the failure itself; it exists in *why* we failed. This is the piece that bosses overlook. They are missing out on the opportunity to learn, just to save a little face.

The reason so many success stories now include the failure piece is because of the value it provides. I often discover that the previous failures my clients endured have enhanced their natural fear of failure. This fear decreases our willingness to take risks. I understand that inherently decreases the chance for failure, but it also prevents us from the massive success that awaits us when we are willing to take those risks.

This is the underlying factor that prevents most of us from finding success. The more we fail, the less likely we are to take the risks leading to success. This is why learning from mistakes is so powerful. With each lesson learned we become smarter. In many cases, the bigger the failure the greater the lesson. Changing a "loss" to a "learn" is empowering. Leaders understand this, and when they bring in their team to help learn the lesson, they are empowering the entire team. You won't always hear about them, but every success story is riddled with failures. Nobody gets it right the first time. The challenge? Being willing to try a second time, and a third time, and a fourth.

The story of bosses and failure is short—they fail and they quit. They may also be apprehensive in attempting anything that involves risk anytime soon. It's a different story with leaders. Leaders are quick to evaluate what went wrong and quick to get back at it. Leaders recognize that failure is going to happen and make provisions. I know this sounds a little crazy, but consider some of the resources we use every day, such as our smart phones. Do you really think that they got smart on the first attempt?

Maybe you have heard of a process called research and development. R&D in any industry is built upon the idea of failure. Test and fail. Test and fail. Test and fail. Test and succeed. I will guarantee it took more than three attempts to create Ibuprofen or an MP4 Player. Why is business any different? Many times the plan does not allow for failure.

When failure happens bosses will identify what went wrong. They may try something else, rather than taking the time to figure out what, where and why it went wrong and what actually might have gone right. Leaders look at the big picture and get much smarter through the process.

When dealing with failure, I've witnessed something that is a clear separator between bosses and leaders: expectation. Bosses present a mission with a declared goal and expect their team to complete that mission and attain the goal. When failure occurs and expectations are not met, bosses immediately want to identify who fell short in the process and who is responsible for the failure. Leaders will present a similar mission, but let the team know there will be challenges along the way. If everyone works together, those challenges can be overcome. When failure occurs, the team jumps in to figure out the needed course corrections, and the process continues.

Make failure your friend. Failure is inevitable, so why run for cover when it happens. Business, just like life, is a moving target. Outside influences, available resources, even the weather are all variables that can change your game plan. Every challenge you overcome today will be one less you have to overcome tomorrow. That is the power in learning from failure. What do you learn by ignoring what has happened? You have a choice. You can *spend* your time trying to identify a different path to your goal, or you can *invest* your time and see what you can learn from the experience.

The most important lesson a leader can learn from failure is this: approaching it as a learning opportunity will enable your followers to do the same. This will keep both you and your followers heading in the right direction.

Are you a BOSS or a LEADER?

A BOSS looks at failure as a loss. A LEADER looks at failure as an opportunity to learn.

A BOSS says failure is not an option. A LEADER acknowledges that failure will occur and by working together to learn and find a better approach, success is possible.

A BOSS blames others or circumstances for failure. A LEADER owns failure, accepts responsibility for it and then pulls their team together to push on toward the goal.

CHAPTER 8

Planning For The Process

"For one to embrace the future, he must first let go of the past. Learn from it and then let it go."

~ BL Smith

Our culture is accustomed to getting what we want, when we want it and how we want it. This has come as a result of technology, education and, to a certain degree, from mastering the art of shortcuts. Yes, I said it—shortcuts. The demand for faster, better, cheaper has pushed us toward success by tackling the major steps, while eliminating as many of the smaller details as possible. I know you can already see where I am going with this. The reason almost everything we do involves a process is because processes identify the steps needed for achievement.

Working with clients for the past seven years as a professional coach has taught me this: as long as we can achieve greater achievements in life and business, we will continually try to figure out easier ways. Allow me to share a valuable lesson. There is no "easy button" on the road to success. Quality takes time and effort and the quickest and most efficient way to success is to follow a process. The challenge comes when we try to eliminate needed steps for the sake of time and available resources. I get it. It's a competitive world out there, and those who wait typically lose out. We have to act now. We can't afford any breakdowns along the way, if we want to finish ahead of the next guy.

Very few struggle with identifying a process, but most are challenged with creating the right one. Bosses will throw together a plan, give it to their team and let them know their deadline. Leaders understand it is not that easy. You might even say there is a process in creating the process. I often share with my clients that they will get out of our relationship what they put into it. Process is no different. Success does not happen in a day, it happens daily. The small details are as important as the bigger ones.

One of my mentors on the John Maxwell Team, Scott Fay, once shared a story about how two small details related to a coffee mug and a belt resulted in one of the most embarrassing moments he ever had to endure. His usual process for getting ready for an airplane flight did not go as planned, and the addition of a coffee mug in his carry-on bag and the absence of a belt around his waist resulted in a pre-flight experience he will never forget. Let's just say he had a hard time getting the bag in the overhead. I'm sure you get the picture.

The point is this: even the smallest of details can make a huge difference. During the Olympics, I am always amazed when the difference between gold and silver, or maybe bronze and no medal at all, comes down to hundredths of a second. Hundredths of a second! Are you kidding me? Do you think any of those athletes felt that if they had followed their process just a little bit better, this difference would have been eradicated? A few seconds may not be that significant in what we are trying to achieve, but we have processes for a reason. We create them to maximize what needs to be done and minimize the potential for leaving out some of the small but critical details.

Often, when working with clients on goal setting activities, I ask the question, "Is that all you need to consider?" Almost every time the answer is, "No" which really confuses me. If someone is sharing their plan, or process, I would think they would have already asked themselves that question. Remember—faster, better, cheaper! Our culture has changed the way we think. Our brains look for the shortcuts. Even when we know there are more steps that need to be considered, we accept the process we have created as good enough. Back to my question, and you will love this. After hearing the "additional" steps needed in the process, I will ask it again. Guess what? The answer is, no. I have sometimes offered this same question three or four times before the client realizes he is not done developing the process until he can answer with a yes.

I am intrigued by the way a boss thinks on the topic of process. There is not enough time to create a comprehensive process that addresses all the issues, but somehow there is always time to clean up the mess when the process fails. I don't think processes fail; I think bosses fail to put the correct process in place. A process is designed to provide an outcome. That outcome does not always have to be success. It can simply provide a confirmation of what you expected to happen. Some processes are actually designed to fail, just to prove the theory that a specific approach will not work, thus eliminating it from the equation. Leaders understand this. A process is a step along the way, and by paying attention to the details you will find the answers you are looking for.

It doesn't matter what profession you are in, the quality of the process you follow will determine the quality of the outcome. I could give you countless examples of colossal failures, but they all come down to one basic element—it was one of the overlooked or ignored smaller details that resulted in failure. The big details, the obvious ones, don't get missed. Even bosses can identify those. The difference is in the details. Leaders realize that the more people they use to develop the process, the more likely they will achieve success. I don't care how good you are, you still only view the world from your set of eyes. Leaders bring their team into the discussion because they know they can't see the entire picture.

Let me share another little secret I have learned along the way. If you want to identify some of those smaller details when creating a successful process, assign some of your team to focus on how the process can fail. This is why these details often get over-looked. The boss, and sometimes the leader, is solely focused on the way to do it right. Sure this is the right approach, but it leaves out the "What if?" oftentimes overlooked by the boss. Put your process to the test before you put it to test. What if? questions are some of my favorites. Many of my clients hate these. "I don't have time to play 'What if?'" I hear that all the time. My response is typically, "Well, you better make time because, "What if?" is going to happen somewhere along the way and you better be ready when it does."

What I just said about putting your process to the test is huge. Challenge the process inside and out. Ask yourself, or your team, if you have covered everything possible. I realize that we are all working on a schedule and have deadlines to meet, but as the saying goes, "Pay me now or pay me later." One way or another, you are going to pay. If you hear someone say, "I know we are not ready, but we have to start!" you are probably listening to a boss. Leaders understand that they can't wait forever, but setting yourself up for failure is the wrong way to get started.

One of the most valuable strengths of a leader is his willingness to identify a process for every part of business and, more importantly, you can't force these processes. Processes take time, resources need to be developed and, in many cases, results are a result of what happens over a specified period of time. Leaders will continually monitor and adjust along the way, but will avoid making changes that will compromise the integrity of the process. Creating the right one in the beginning and allowing enough time for the process to function as designed, are crucial in achieving your desired results.

Are you a BOSS or a LEADER?

A BOSS makes decisions that will expedite the process by taking shortcuts. A LEADER will monitor and make adjustments along the way but not deviate from the original plan.

A BOSS tries to eliminate minor details that will delay the process. A LEADER acknowledges that the details, even the small ones, are critical to allow the process to take its required course.

A BOSS provides the process to his or her team and waits for the results. A LEADER allows their team to develop the process and involves them in navigating the course.

CHAPTER 9

———— ❧ ————

The Relevance Of Respect

"One of the most sincere forms of respect is actually listening to what another has to say."

~ Bryant H. McGill

On the surface, this one is easy: bosses demand respect, leaders earn it. The bigger picture is much more complicated. Certainly there are positions that require respect, i.e., corporate executives, political leaders, etc. Even the position of a boss requires respect. When it comes to dealing with business leaders, the problem I often deal with occurs when the person, "the boss," has not earned the respect required by the position.

It is important to point out that there is a big difference between not respecting someone and disrespecting them. Simply put, you should never disrespect anyone. If you feel like you have been disrespected by a superior, he was probably a boss. If a leader has an issue with someone, he will deal with it respectfully, looking for ways to improve the situation. Leaders don't disrespect other people; it shows a lack of leadership on their part.

The real challenge is respecting someone who hasn't earned it. We have all been around the water cooler at work and heard employees badmouth a superior. My guess is you have been one of them. I know I have in the past.

There are many different levels of respect and I want to focus on a few of them. The first is what respect means to your business. When you run a respectable business, you send the message that you have a certain set of standards by which you operate. Many of the businesses I work with have their standards posted throughout the building. If you advertise it, you better stand behind it. Respect is typically a top-down dynamic in the workplace. Well respected leaders usually have well respected followers, and followers who respect others. This can work the opposite way as well. If the boss is not well respected the organizational culture follows suit.

When you hear the phrase "a well-respected business" what comes to mind? My response is: an organization with strong leaders. Let me ask you to consider another question: How often is the word respect even used in your workplace? It doesn't surprise me that bosses tend stay away from the topic. Most bosses know they have respect issues and simply avoid them because they know they are not respected by their peers or their followers. Gaining the respect of others takes time and sacrifice, which is another reason why bosses avoid the issue. The time element is easy to figure out but the sacrifice needed may have you a little puzzled. The reason that gaining respect takes sacrifice is because people respect those who put the interests of others first. They gain respect by making decisions that serve the whole, not just themselves.

People look up to, or admire, those whom they respect. We all know people we desire to be more like and, in most cases, they are leaders; very seldom are they bosses.

By now you should understand the difference between bosses and leaders. Want a quick test? How much do you respect them? Respect is easy to identify but difficult to develop. Here's another quick test: Does the individual have followers? I realize I have used people, followers and employees pretty loosely throughout, but the bottom line is that only people who have loyal followers are leaders.

I used to believe that certain positions required respect. After studying this topic for several years, I see a big difference between being respectful and actually respecting someone. Having someone respect you really doesn't amount to much if they don't have respect *for* you. Outside of the military, you don't see the requirement to address someone as sir very often. Yet bosses love to be addressed that way. It's a sign of respect, right? It is, but that's all it is. How many leaders do you know who ask to be addressed as sir? Not many I know of. That is a positional sir. Leaders are more concerned with the personal sir.

The most basic way to earn respect is to follow the golden rule: treat others as you would like to be treated. If you are a boss and are reading this, don't expect things to change overnight. Respect is built over time and is only achieved when your followers trust you. Trust is another topic we will spend some time on later in the book, but is an important part of respect. They almost go hand in hand. Bosses are rarely trusted and rarely respected. Leaders, on the other hand, are both trusted and respected.

Let's take a look at what happens when your people don't respect you. First, they are going to be looking out for themselves because they know you won't. When that happens, their entire work performance becomes centered on what's best for them, not the organization, and definitely not you. Even worse than what they do, or don't do, is what they say. I know I said you should never disrespect anyone, but I will assume that if you are reading this, you live in the real world. You know what happens. You know what gets said behind the boss's back. The end result is dysfunction and lack of unity. Does this sound like the type of team that you want to be a part of? Does this sound like a team that will perform at a high level? It's no wonder bosses collect a paycheck while leaders earn one.

Let's consider what happens when your followers respect you. They enjoy performing at a high level, knowing their actions will make you look good and you, in turn, will make them look good. They also show up ready to engage and be part of the success story because they know you will make them part of it. *You earn respect by showing respect* and when bosses figure this out, they can begin their journey to becoming a leader.

*****

I am always looking for tips for leadership development. Here is an article on some great ways to earn respect.

7 WAYS TO EARN RESPECT AS A LEADER

Do you wonder why some people naturally gain respect, while others have to command or, worse, demand it?

Earning respect is in direct correlation to treating others with the same. Showing respect sounds like a basic skill, and yet somehow complaints about being disrespected run rampant around coffee rooms and bathrooms in companies around the country.

Are parents and teachers shirking their responsibility for turning everyone into good little citizens that can play well with others? Perhaps, but more likely, cultural norms have changed. Families allow for greater familiarity, and schools are more focused on test scores and class sizes than they are on teaching little Johnny and Susie to stand out as leaders.

But whether you are the executive in charge or a contributing team member, your ability to earn respect will impact your emotional happiness and ultimate career trajectory. Some people in authority believe they are entitled to respect simply due to their position or experience, but this sort of respect diminishes over time and can ultimately hurt the company culture.

Here are seven tips to help you be a leader who earns respect rather than just demands it.

1. Be consistent.

If you find you lack credibility, it's probably because you are saying one thing and doing another. People do pay attention to what you say until you give them reason not to by doing the opposite. You don't have to be predictable, just don't be a hypocrite.

2. Be punctual.

Nothing makes me lose respect for someone more than being made to wait. Time is the most valuable commodity for successful people. Missing appointments or being late demonstrates a total disregard for the lives and needs of others. Get control of your calendar.

3. Be responsive.

The challenge with contact management today is there are too many ways to communicate. Between Twitter, Facebook, Messenger, text, phone, Skype, and Facetime, people are in a quandary to know what is the best way to reach you. And even with all the channels, some people still don't respond in a timely manner, leaving colleagues hanging or chasing them. Limit your channels and respond within 24 hours if you want to appear communication worthy.

4. Be right much of the time, but be comfortable being wrong.

The simple way to be right is to do your homework and state facts that are well thought out. Still, you may have to make a best guess now and then even when information is too scarce to know for sure. Take it as a qualified risk, manage expectations, and if you're wrong, smile and be happy you learned something that day.

5. Forgive others and yourself for mistakes.

If you're not erring, you're not trying. Healthy leaders encourage experimentation and create environments of safe failure. Encourage people to take mitigated risks, and set an example for how to shake off a failure and bounce back.

6. Show respect to others when they are wrong and right.

Disparaging people who make errors will reflect worse on you than those who err. On the flip side, any jealous tendencies toward those who succeed will surely be noticed by those around. Live as if in a glass body. Assume all can see inside your heart.

7. Help those who are holding you back, but not too much.

Good leaders help those around them succeed by overcoming weakness. But respect is lost quickly for the boss who placates habitual troublemakers at the expense of the group's success. Know when to support weak players, and cut them loose when they clearly hamper the result.

Too many people today assume leadership positions without consideration for their impact on others. The leadership vacuum in business today allows them to stay as long they manage acceptable results. Ultimately, your personal leadership legacy will not be remembered for your M.B.A., your sales numbers, or the toys you acquired. Most likely, it will be the positive, personal impact you created, one follower at a time.[5]

*****

Don't make the mistake of thinking your accomplishments, your skills and especially your position will earn you respect. It doesn't work that way. Respect is an unwritten rule and when a boss demands respect he's breaking that rule. Rules are created so we know where the boundaries are for what we are doing. We either conform or we don't. Respect isn't black and white, that's why it's an unwritten rule. Leaders and their followers don't get hung up on rules, they just perform. Bosses spend a lot of time talking about rules. What you should do, what you shouldn't. Isn't it interesting that when there is mutual respect between a leader and his followers, the rules are rarely an issue?

Start acting worthy of the respect you desire and your followers will respond in kind. One final thought on respect: the less respect is talked about the better. Spending a lot of time discussing the topic generally means there is a problem or, in more direct terms, a lack of respect. Just a thought….

Are you a BOSS or a LEADER?

A BOSS asks people to show respect. A LEADER earns their respect and doesn't need to ask for it.

A BOSS believes respect is about the position. A LEADER knows respect is about the person.

A BOSS looks for others to respect him or her before they will respect them. A LEADER shows respect to others first in an effort to earn the respect they desires.

CHAPTER 10

---※---

Playing Safe With Consistency

"Leadership can't be fabricated. If it is fabricated and rehearsed, you can't fool the guys in the locker room. So when you talk about leadership, it comes with performance. Leadership comes with consistency."

~ Junior Seau

Earlier, I discussed how the impact of losing control can stress us out and decrease our ability to focus. If you want to mess with the control people have over their own thoughts and emotions, start being inconsistent in what you do and what you say. There is something in all of us that desires the unexpected. Who doesn't love an occasional surprise? But in our day-to-day existence, consistency is crucial to staying in control.

Consistency provides stability and security. Those two words give us peace of mind. Your people understand things happen. Sometimes they are good things, sometimes bad;

but it's not the event that creates the stress, it's how you deal with it. There is a clear difference between leaders and bosses when it comes to being consistent. Leaders are more consistent when life happens because they respond to the circumstance or condition that presents itself. Bosses deal with the same challenges that leaders do but *they don't respond, they react.*

Think about this. When a leader responds to a situation, he is staying in control of his actions and making the best decision moving forward. He is not letting the situation determine his course of action. When a boss reacts, he is letting the circumstance determine the next move. Do you see the difference?

The most common failure I have seen when it comes to consistency, or the lack thereof, is in the planning stage. I have seen many plans fail because they were built upon the belief that most, or all, of the variables could be controlled. Neither life nor business works like that. We eventually get thrown a curve ball we did not prepare for and, due to a lack of proper planning, we react instead of respond.

Pat Summit, former head coach of the University of Tennessee Lady Volunteer basketball team, used to leave the locker room for a period during the half-time intermission to allow her players to answer three questions on a chalk board: (1.) What did we do right? (2.) What did we do wrong? and (3.) What do we need to do differently? What if your team answered those questions every time they faced a challenge? Summit is well recognized as a great leader. By running her girls through this exercise, she empowered them to formulate their response in the second half. Being the winningest NCAA basketball coach in college history, men or women, is not just due to her longevity as a coach. Summit brought a consistent game plan each and every time her team hit the court. That consistency provided control for her teams.

Responding beats reacting every time. Even our emergency services understand this. Phrases like "response time" or "responding to an accident" are used in lieu of react. They understand the difference. Did you ever notice that bosses are a little harder to find in our critical response industries?

As a coach, I pride myself on being a great listener; I listen to the words my clients use. The words respond and react tell me a lot about the mindset of my clients, often leading to some very interesting and productive conversations. Strong leaders can respond on-the-fly in most situations. This is because they had a strong plan to begin with and anticipated making adjustments along the way. This is what separates leaders and bosses. Follow me on this.

When a leader maintains control and responds to a specific situation, the main objective does not change. Everything continues to point toward the predetermined goal. When a boss reacts, he or she deviates from the goal by reacting instead of responding. Even if for a short time, he steps out from the path leading to the goal. The result is inconsistent behavior because the circumstances are usually completely different. Each time something comes up, the boss reacts in a different way and compromises the security and stability he should be providing.

I never really differentiated between these two words until I realized the difference in the resulting outcomes. Security and stability are two of the greatest needs we have as humans and consistency provides both. Remember, the performance of your people will be impacted by the amount of focus they can place on the task at hand. If they are worried about future decisions related to their job or the longevity of the business, their focus will be in the wrong place.

Focus and clarity are major factors in the overall performance and productivity of your people. Both of these improve when distractions are kept to a minimum. Consistency eliminates some of the issues we inherently think about during any given day.

I once heard that powerful questions can't go unanswered in your mind. Your brain fixates on the question until an answer is found or until a new distraction replaces it. Bosses add noise and clutter. Leaders take measures to eliminate the distractions and create an environment that promotes clarity and focus. Consistency suggests that things will remain the same. When things are the same, we don't spend time thinking about them and it is much easier to focus.

Time is constant. It is the one commodity we can't get any more of; whatever we do in an eight hour day will fit into those eight hours. Over the years, I have suggested something to many of my clients that you might find useful as well. Here are four questions I like to ask, related to time management: (1.) What do you need to start? (2.) What do you need to stop? (3.) What do you need to do less of? (4.) What do you need to do more of? Let me show you the difference between how leaders and bosses address these questions.

Very few of us have a lot of free time. In fact, most of us wake up each morning with more on our list than we will even have a chance to complete that day. The only way to add an activity is to remove something else. There is a sequence to those four questions that may seem insignificant but will have a huge impact on consistency. If there is no room in the schedule, something needs to be removed to make room. Bosses don't get this. They pile on more work and then wait to see what doesn't get done. Does this sound like a way to maintain consistency?

A leader will take a look at what needs to be done, then eliminate the lowest priority item to make room for something of greater importance. The result is that followers can continue on with their work without being distracted. When the new item is introduced, it simply drops into the allotted time created when the other activity was removed. This is a much smoother process and creates much less disruption. This works for the stop and start questions and the more or less questions. Do this the wrong way and your people will mentally check out from what they are doing, and focus on how they are going to complete the added tasks. Do this the right way and your followers won't have to think about how they are going to get the additional activities completed. More stability, more security, more control, all while remaining consistent.

I will close this chapter with this thought. In order to be consistent, you need to have systems in place to carry out the specific duties your job description requires. Systems are your playbook for success. That playbook will include predefined plans for various activities. When you have an activity to perform, grab your playbook and lay out the plan. That playbook will allow you to consistently apply proven methods to complete your work. What's in your playbook?

Are you a BOSS or a LEADER?

A BOSS reacts to a situation and allows the situation to determine the next step. A LEADER responds to a situation and determines the next course of action while keeping the focus on the original goal.

A BOSS tells you to, "Make time for it." A LEADER knows that people can't 'make time' and schedules the activities to fit into the time that he or she has.

A BOSS adds tasks, then waits to see what doesn't get done. A LEADER removes the lowest priority activities before adding new ones, which maintains consistency.

CHAPTER 11

———— ✦ ————

Winning With Competition

*"The healthiest competition occurs when average
people win by putting in above average effort."*

~ Colin Powell

This chapter is a discussion about competition and
collaboration and how bosses and leaders incorporate
them into their business. Previous generations were a
collaborative society. Over the past several decades, the
demand for production and a reduction in manual labor
has moved us to a competitive society. This has extended
to even the lowest levels of our workforce. Our value is
determined not by the work that is accomplished, but by
how we compete compared our co-workers.

This reality in the workplace has created a situation
in which we are forced to *appear* more valuable than the
next guy. Do you see the problem? Teamwork still exists
but it looks much different than it used to. Sports are a

great example. Forty years ago, it was not uncommon for a professional athlete to spend his entire career in the same city playing for the same team. Today, players get moved around before the fans even get to know who they are. Consider the automobile. How long do you own your car before trading it in for a new model? Business is no different. Same job, different company. I have seen it happen over and over again. Organizations wonder why there is such high turnover. Everyone is looking for the next best opportunity because the competitive spirit is alive and well.

I am not going to suggest we don't need a competitive spirit, but it has become an either/or with a collaborative spirit instead of an in-addition-to. This is true, at least in businesses run by bosses. Once upon a time we combined a competitive spirit with a collaborative effort. Leaders understand that a combination of the two is the best pathway to success. There is no doubt competition is a much needed part of any business, but it should not be between co-workers. Unfortunately, far too many businesses have created this environment.

One of the topics I often discuss with my clients is that of team unity. I like to ask, "Would you consider your work place competitive or collaborative?" I usually get the deer-in-the-headlights look. No problem. Now we have a great topic to explore. After a few minutes, I get typical responses suggesting that competition is with other businesses and that collaboration exists within the walls of their business. Then I take it a little further and ask whether they feel their employees are competing with each other for their jobs.

I recognize those who work hard should be rewarded and those who don't perform need to find another job. But if you think back to the comments I made relative to the cost of employee turnover, you might see the bigger issue. We want the best employees to rise to the top by performing at a higher level than their counterparts. Then we get frustrated because we are hiring and firing all the time. Bosses do a lot of hiring and firing. Leaders realize that if you can build a strong, performing team through both collaboration and competition, the company will succeed and there will be less employee turnover.

Here is what many of my clients have discovered when embracing the idea that it is possible for followers, achieving at differing levels, to co-exist and to do so productively. The high achievers actually inspire the lower achievers to step-up their game. Most people realize if they don't perform, their tenure will soon come to an end. With no one to offer inspiration to raise their own performance, unknowingly, these people are waiting for the day when they have two checks in their envelope. Leaders take a look at the chemistry of their team and put together groups of people who will collectively perform at a higher level than they would individually. Let's jump back to the sports world again. Have you noticed that most often it is the best team that wins, not the team with the best players? It's the teams with members who collaborate together with a competitive spirit that end up holding the trophy.

The reason is, "We is always greater than me." A team working together will always outperform the combined individual efforts of those on the team. Leaders recognize the power of combining strengths and create a mix of individuals within a team that provides all the tools needed for achievement. Bosses will create teams based on availability and schedule and do no more than hope it works out. When it is apparent that one team member is underperforming, they will be quick to replace; whereas a leader will make an effort to bring the team together and strengthen any visible weak link. When a team actually overcomes adversity and grows in the process, it is empowering and inspires the team to achieve even more than what was originally expected.

Today's leaders are bringing back the collaborative, competitive spirit and doing it with the same group of people. Bosses continue to sit back and watch the top performers rise to the top and replace the underachievers. Many times this backfires because eventually those top performers move on; they realize they are working for a boss and want to follow a leader. In some instances within a company, the top performer becomes the leader, then the boss gets two checks.

While some people are not cut out for the job or position they have been assigned, they can't expect their coworkers to carry them. Leaders will invest the time to try to find the right fit, only letting someone go as a last resort. Bosses are not willing to invest the time and continue to lean heavily on their top performers for production. This is another reason top performers don't last long with bosses. Leaders provide an opportunity for their followers to succeed but understand there may come a time when it is better for the team to let go of those who do not fit. The decision is based on the individual, not necessarily on the numbers. Leaders see their followers as people. Bosses see their people as resources. There is a big difference.

The biggest mistake businesses make when identifying those who will fit into a collaborative, competitive environment is often made during recruitment. As much as we like to believe we hire people based on their resumes, leaders know they are getting the entire package, including baggage. Bosses, however, are quick to hire. When they are short-handed, they grab the first qualified person and put them to work. Remember our discussion on character when I stated only ten percent of who you are is related to your skills? Most resumes don't include much more than a list of skills and qualifications.

Before you hire someone, it is best to spend some time together before introducing them to your team. Then ask your team, the ones with whom they will be working, for their thoughts. Ask about topics such as vision and purpose. You might be surprised by some of the responses. I have had many of my clients tell me they knew right away whether or not an individual would fit in after getting to know them. Don't you think it makes sense to invest a little more time on the front end rather than a lot more on the back end?

Let all of your followers know you want them to keep that competitive edge while reminding them they are an extension of each other. They will then be more likely to perform to the set expectations.

Are you a BOSS or a LEADER?

A BOSS is quick to hire, quick to fire. A LEADER is slow to hire and only lets someone go when all other options have been exhausted.

A BOSS promotes individual accomplishment and compares their people to each other. A LEADER rewards team success and encourages their followers to support each other in a collaborative effort.

A BOSS puts together a team based on schedule and availability with little regard to chemistry. A LEADER strives to put together a team that will work together and complement each other with their respective strengths.

CHAPTER 12

---❧---

Wired For Responsibility

"You must take personal responsibility. You cannot change the circumstances, the seasons, or the wind, but you can change yourself. That is something you have charge of."

~ Jim Rohn

Responsibility is an interesting topic. Some believe it's about what you *need* to do, while others believe it's about what you *did*. In reality it's about both, but leaders and bosses look at each very differently. As far as what has already been done, bosses take credit for wins and place blame for losses. Leaders, by comparison, share the victories and own the losses. I recognize there is an in-between, but if you put this to the test you will find it fairly accurate.

Here is the major difference between bosses and leaders regarding responsibility: bosses are responsible *for* something and leaders are responsible *to* someone. This is supported by my assertion that bosses manage things and leaders lead people. There is a difference between leading people and being a leader. Bosses will occasionally exhibit leadership skills but in the end are still managing things. They are responsible for an outcome but not the personal development or success of any individuals. We will further explore the complexities of responsibility, but this is the way it breaks down in the most basic way.

The most common issue related to who is responsible for what is that bosses resist accepting responsibility when things go wrong. They are quick to blame and look for circumstances or other people to accuse. The real tragedy is, by not owning the outcome, they fail to see failure as an opportunity to learn. All their effort is spent on trying to determine who made the mistakes, when they should be trying to understand what went wrong and what lessons can be learned.

Leaders understand that failure does not have to be a loss. By taking responsibility for the negative outcome, they can control the way in which their team or organization can move forward. While the boss is playing defense, trying to justify what went wrong, the leader will go on offense and plan the next course of action. There is a common saying in the sports world: a good defense will usually win out. I believe that to be true. The reason is that when the clock expires the game is over. By definition, defense is designed to eliminate forward progress. The result of a good defense in business is nothing more than standing still. And everyone knows how long a business will exist by standing still.

Going on the offense, on the other hand, is all about forward motion to reach a specific goal The desired outcome for any business is also to reach their goals.

Now let's take a look at being responsible for what hasn't happened yet. As previously stated, bosses are responsible for such things as deadlines, profit margins, product launches or completion projects. Bosses are capable of achieving them, and doing so successfully. Leaders also shine in these areas but there is a big difference in the way they do so. Leaders take on the responsibility to provide opportunities that allow their followers to become successful along the way to completing an activity.

Taking responsibility for your actions or your people requires the willingness to take ownership in the results. Leaders take responsibility for both the good and bad and, when needed, seek help in identifying what it will take to play a more significant role in developing those around them. Leaders are responsible for the people they are leading, and recognize that focusing on the personal development of their followers is the pathway to success.

Bosses, however, want to know how to solve problems instead of developing followers who will avoid them in the first place.

I don't think I fully understood how important the topic of responsibility was until I started coaching. Blame—the antithesis of taking responsibility—is like a poison that can take down a business in the blink of an eye. It can undermine years of effort in building businesses, partnerships and relationships. When an individual is unwilling to take responsibility for an outcome, someone else is forced to. And that other person will probably not appreciate the position they've been put in. One thing leads to another, and in a short amount of time everything goes up in smoke. After seeing this happen a few times, I began to understand why leaders are willing take responsibility for the outcome, whether they were responsible for it or not. Taking responsibility is the way to control the process. Leaders want that responsibility because they know it's the only way they can make sure they are part of the solution.

If you want to be a leader, there are times you will have to give up your rights to a "fair trial." It's just the way leadership works. You have to give up to go up, and sometimes you have to give up more so that others can go up with you. The principle to understand is that everyone is going up. You might be wondering how failure can result in everyone going up. That's because leaders invest in their people and work with them to accomplish what they set out to achieve. When things go wrong, there is no blame, just a desire to correct the problem. The spectators in this scenario see a group of people taking responsibility for the outcome, seeking a solution to fix what went wrong. People respect that type of behavior and respect and trust those who demonstrate it.

Don't make the mistake of thinking all you have to do is say, "It was my fault." and all will be forgiven. Leaders work very hard investing in their followers, putting together solid plans and developing a track record of success. When things do go wrong, there is an expectation the situation will be rectified. Bosses simply accept the fact that you win some, you lose some and hopefully it will turn out better next time. *Don't be a boss, be a leader.*

*****

Brian Tracy is one of the all-time gurus regarding leadership. Here is a summary from his book.

THE 7 RESPONSIBILITIES OF LEADERSHIP

There are seven basics that never change, the key responsibilities of leadership in any organization. On a scale of 1 to 10, your ability in each of these seven areas determines your value to yourself and your contribution to your organization. Here they are:

Your First Responsibility: Set and Achieve Business Goals

The number-one reason for business and executive failure is the inability to achieve the sales, growth, and profitability goals for which the leader is responsible. Setting and achieving business goals embraces every part of strategic and market planning, including products, services, people, productivity, promotion, finances, and competitive responses.

The Second Responsibility of Leadership: Innovate and Market

As Peter Drucker said, the purpose of a business is to "create and keep a customer."

Only through continuous innovation of products, services, processes, and promotional methods can companies create and keep customers. As Bruce Henderson of the Boston Consulting Group wrote, "All strategic planning is market planning."

The Third Responsibility of Leadership: Solve Problems and Make Decisions

Remember, a goal unachieved is merely a problem unsolved. A sales target unachieved is a problem unsolved. The only obstacles that stand between you and the business success you desire are problems, difficulties, hindrances, and barriers. Your ability to go over, under, or around these problems is central to your success.

The Fourth Responsibility of Leadership: Set Priorities and Focus on Key Tasks

One of the most important jobs you do is to deploy limited resources, especially of people and money, into those areas where they can make the greatest contribution to the success of the enterprise.

The law of the excluded alternative says, "Doing one thing means not doing something else."

Time is your scarcest resource. It is limited, perishable, irretrievable, and irreplaceable. The way you allocate your time can be the critical determinant of everything you achieve—or fail to achieve.

The Fifth Responsibility of Leadership: Be a Role Model to Others

Albert Schweitzer once wrote, "You must teach men at the school of example, for they will learn at no other."

Throughout the ages, the example that you establish in your character, attitude, personality, and work habits, and especially the way you treat other people, sets the tone for your department or organization.

You do not raise morale in an organization; it always filters down from the top. There are no bad soldiers under a good general.

One of the great questions for you to continually ask yourself is, "What kind of a company would my company be if everyone in it was just like me?"

Marshall Goldsmith, top executive coach for senior executives in the Fortune 1000, has demonstrated over the years that a single change in a behavioral characteristic of a key executive can cause a positive multiplier effect that impacts the behavior of an enormous number of people.

Leaders conduct themselves as though everyone is watching, even when no one is watching.

The Sixth Responsibility of Leadership: Persuade, Inspire, and Motivate Others to Follow You

Tom Peters said that the best leaders don't create followers, they create leaders. It's true that you want your people to have initiative and the liberty to act on that initiative. But all initiatives must be in the support and service of what you are trying to achieve as a leader.

If people aren't following you, you are not a leader. If no one is listening to you, believes you, or cares what you say, you are not going to succeed. If people are only going through the motions to earn a paycheck, the greatest business strategy in the world will fail.

You must motivate others to follow your vision, to support and achieve the goals and objectives that you have set, to buy into the mission of the organization as you see it. Today, getting others to follow you takes more than command and control. You have to earn their trust, respect, and confidence. That is the key to sustainable success as a leader.

The Seventh Responsibility of Leadership: Perform and Get Results

In the final analysis, your ability to get the results that are expected of you is the critical factor that determines your success.[6]

*****

There are definitely times when taking responsibility is easy. But if you want the best from your followers, and the best possible outcome when things do go wrong, start owning everything you do. Blame does not accomplish anything; in fact, it makes things worse. The people you should be concerned with are the ones who want to know what the solution is, not the ones who want to know who was responsible for the problem. Those are the people who want to know who to blame. Bosses always want to know whose fault it was because as long as it wasn't theirs, they think they look better by establishing fault. In reality, the only ones they look better than are the other people playing the same blame game.

Are you a BOSS or a LEADER?

A BOSS is responsible for something. A LEADER is responsible to someone.

A BOSS tries to gain credibility by showing who was at fault. A LEADER gives up to go up and sets their followers up for success in the process.

A BOSS blames others when something goes wrong. A LEADER takes responsibility, no matter who was at fault, and immediately looks for ways to right the ship.

CHAPTER 13

---✦---

Turning Accountability Into Action

> *"A body of men holding themselves accountable to nobody ought not be trusted by anybody."*
>
> ~ *Thomas Paine*

I follow a number of thought leaders on the topics of leadership and personal development. One theme I hear from most of them is that of accountability. Unfortunately, I have rarely seen this word used to describe what is actually taking place. One of my mentors emphasizes three key elements in any success story: awareness, intentionality and accountability. Although the focus of this chapter will be on the latter, it's important to understand the process we go through in achieving success at any level.

Everything we do starts with awareness that we can accomplish a goal. As we move through life and expand our knowledge, we discover new opportunities toward which we should be moving. To move forward we need to set the intention to do so. That's pretty simple. I have heard it said that the greatest gap we will face in life is the gap between what we know and what we do. Uh oh! Many of my clients are well educated, yet one simple little item is often what keeps them from the success they desire. What is that one little thing? You guessed it. Accountability.

I used to believe the saying, "Knowledge is power." Then I realized knowledge is worthless unless you do something with it. That gap I just spoke of, the gap between what you know and what you do, is what separates success and failure. Yoda said it best, "There is no try, there is only do and do not." I cringe every time I hear the word *try*. What does it really mean anyway? "They didn't try hard enough." "We need to try harder." "I will try and get better." Let me ask you a question. How much is enough, harder or better? Unless we are held accountable to a specific, measurable and time-constrained action, it's not going to happen. I know some of you are very successful at staying on task and checking items off your list. I also know there are some items, items that continue to remain on your list, which you have not completed. Why?

We simply don't have the power to hold ourselves accountable for the items on our list that are hard. You know those items you don't tell anyone about because you know you probably won't accomplish them. We all have them. *If you want to change your outcome, change your plan.* Reach out to someone who won't be afraid to call you out, tell you what you need to hear and then hold you accountable.

*****

Here is a great sports story on the importance of accountability:

ARMANDO GALARRAGA

June 2, 2010. Armando Galarraga, a pitcher for the Detroit Tigers, was one out from pitching a perfect game; something that is rare in major league baseball. However, on the last out the first base umpire Jim Joyce ruled the runner safe, putting an end to Galarraga's quest for a perfect game. Joyce believed he made the right call until he saw the replay for himself after the game; the replays showed the runner was clearly out and that Galarraga should have got credit for a perfect game. Joyce, the umpire, immediately went to the 28-year-old pitcher from Venezuela after the game and apologized for getting the call wrong.

Galarraga then turned around and forgave him for blowing a call that cost him something he may never do again: throw a perfect game. "He probably feels more bad than me," Galarraga said. "Nobody's perfect. Everybody's human. I understand. I give the guy a lot of credit for saying, 'I need to talk to you.' You don't see an umpire tell you that after a game. I gave him a hug."[7]

*****

You've got to love it when people are accountable. Accountability is all about doing the right thing because it's the right thing to do. When we own up to our mistakes, we garner immense respect.

There are two sides of accountability—being held accountable and holding someone else accountable. Bosses and leaders act very differently in both. Bosses hate being held accountable because it represents commitment and having somebody check up on them. Leaders don't mind being held accountable; in fact, they invite it. Leaders realize that being held accountable will take them to the next level, helping them achieve things they can't achieve on their own. They also welcome the opportunity to hold their followers accountable for the same reasons.

Accountability is most commonly implemented in the fitness industry. Working out consistently is something many struggle to do. I doubt if the idea of accountability started in the gym, but it has definitely found a home there. People who go to a gym know that what they are attempting is going to be hard without someone to whom they will be accountable.

I am sure this isn't breaking news for you but understand this—even though the process is fairly straightforward, few of us use it. We don't want to be vulnerable. We don't want to risk failing. After all, how much trouble do you get into when the only person who knows you failed is you? That's why self-accountability rarely works. When we tell someone that we are going to accomplish a goal, and know they will be checking up, something happens inside our head that helps us succeed. It might be because we don't want to disappoint the person who is holding us accountable; or fail in front of them; or it might be because we are a little more driven to prove to others we could do whatever it was. In any case, it was accountability that led to the success.

If you want people to follow you, give them a reason. Show them you are vulnerable enough to get help in the areas in which you are weak. This doesn't make you look weak, it makes you look strong. Go a step further. Offer to hold others accountable in something in which they have been struggling. I coach high level executives every day and part of what I provide is accountability. Everyone struggles with something, even the most successful people.

Bosses won't hold people accountable; they just tell employees what to do and expect them will do it. I think they are missing an opportunity to not only make their better but also make themselves look better; employee output is a reflection of who they are. Leaders jump at the chance to hold their followers accountable because it makes everyone better. If you want to create a band of followers, give them the opportunity and means to accomplish more than they ever thought possible. Not only will they reach new levels of accomplishment, but they will have you, in part, to thank for it.

There is a catch in providing accountability for someone. The easy part is checking in to confirm they are accomplishing their goals. The hard part comes when they fall short. This is where your commitment really matters, especially if you are a leader. The first thing you need to do is determine why the failure occurred. It is important to learn from what prevented their success. Then help identify what needs to change in order for the individual to succeed. You may need to repeat your words until the person either fully understands or it becomes clear that the individual does not really want it badly enough. You can't fix that. You can only help those willing to help themselves.

Don't make the mistake of believing you can do everything on your own. It is much easier to come up with reasons why you can't do something than why you can. Time and money are the two biggest reasons we don't accomplish what we set out to do. They are easy excuses. Easy excuses don't fly with accountability partners. The person holding you accountable will recognize your reasons or, more accurately stated, excuses every time. The bottom line is *if you could do it yourself, you would have already done it.* You will have to stretch. It might even hurt a little, but that's how you grow.

Bosses leave their people to take care of themselves. Leaders understand that helping their followers achieve great things will empower them to believe they can achieve even more. Get your team together and ask everyone to come up with one thing they have been unsuccessful at achieving, then partner each person up for accountability. Do this as a team, and you will end up with the entire team holding each other accountable. You will get great results and build team unity at the same time. More important than that, you will build your people.

Are you a BOSS or a LEADER?

A BOSS avoids accountability like the plague. A LEADER will not only seek it out but offer it to their followers as well.

A BOSS will provide countless reasons why it can't be done. A LEADER will challenge their entire team to answer the question, "How can I?" and then hold them accountable.

A BOSS tries to fill the gap between what we know and what we do with more information. A LEADER closes that gap through awareness, intentionality and accountability.

CHAPTER 14

———— ⚜ ————

Developing The Right Strategy

"The essence of strategy is choosing what not to do."

~ Michael Porter

A great strategy coupled with great execution will give you great results. A great strategy with poor execution will leave you wondering what went wrong. The wrong strategy, no matter how good the execution, will almost always end poorly. So on the surface, it would appear that if you have a great strategy and execute well, you should achieve great results. Sounds pretty straight forward in concept. So how come it doesn't always turn out that way? The majority of the time it is in the execution. I am sure most of you have heard the expression, "It works on paper." referring to a plan that, by design, should work. But it doesn't always work out in the real world. Strategies are like that as well. Most of the time they do work on paper before the execution phase begins, then something goes wrong while executing.

I would never suggest that bosses are not competent. They just lack the required skills or character to be a leader. Bosses are more than capable of designing solid strategies that "work on paper." Then comes the execution phase. This is where a big difference between bosses and leaders shows up. Execution of a strategy requires the involvement of people. Empowered followers will be executing the strategy of a leader, while whoever is available will be calling the shots for a boss.

I'm sure you would agree that investing the necessary time to come up with a good strategy is a good use of available resources. The problem comes from not selecting the *right* people or team to execute the plan. The subtitle of this book, *How to Turn Your Employees into Followers*, is built upon the premise that not all of your employees are following you. If they are not following you, how can you expect them to execute with accuracy and integrity on your behalf? Bosses might have a group of people working under or for them, but leaders have people working with them. Do you see the difference?

Any discussion about strategy has to include an analysis of the available resources used to execute the plan. Just because your employees have a pulse that doesn't mean they are the correct resource for the job. One of the most common mistakes I have observed while working with my clients is choosing the wrong resources to execute the plan. Following that is failing to identify all the needed resources to begin with. You need to understand that people are going to be at the top of the list when identifying the needed resources to execute the plan. Let me share another one of my little secrets with you: *Your people will invest into their jobs what you invest into them.*

Another one of my favorite questions concerning the use of people is, "What's in it for them?" The typical answers include a paycheck and job security. That's the mindset of a boss. This chapter is about more than just a strategic plan to run and build your business. It's about creating a strategy to develop followers. People don't follow because of a paycheck or job security. They can get those by simply working hard and staying out of trouble. If you want followers, you need to develop them. If you have a great strategy for developing your people, you won't need to look for followers; they will be lining up at your doorstep. I'm sure you have seen or heard about businesses that have been recognized as "the most desired place to work." Do you think you will find bosses or leaders running these companies?

I am going to spend the remainder of this chapter answering four of my favorite questions related to developing a strategy that will turn your employees into followers. Let's start with…

"What do you need to stop?" You need to stop believing that your people are financially motivated and perform based on the location of a decimal point. Some of them will be, but honestly, if that's what motivates them, you need to seriously consider whether they belong on your team. Stop offering more perks and benefits as a trade for hours. This will result in highly motivated employees who will eventually burn out or take on more than they can competently handle. because they want that next pay increase, a bigger office, an assigned parking spot or another week of paid vacation. Let's move to…

"What do you need to start?" Start changing the way you think. It has been said that if you keep doing what you've been doing, you'll keep getting what you've been getting. I'm going to assume you would like to change at least some of what you've been getting. When you change the way you look at your people, your people begin to look different. They are no longer only resources but individuals who desire to be part of a greater cause. You can also accomplish this by bringing them inside your protected circle. Let them help create the future. If you want to see an engaged, inspired, employee, then give them a reason to be one. Make your people feel valued. They will value their jobs and maybe even you. Followers are going to invest their time and energy in a leader who is open to new ideas and the opinions. Change is required to advance. The "way we used to do things" is a recipe for disaster. Leaders are always looking for new and creative ways to initiate change. Now we explore…

"**What do you need to do more of?**" Spend more time with your people. If you want people to follow you, they need to get to know you. Additionally, take more interest in each person. I can certainly understand why it's important to know what they do, but getting to know who they are is the way to really connect. Let me ask you a couple of questions. Do you know the name of their spouse? Do you know the names and ages of their children? Do you acknowledge them on their birthday? One of the greatest needs of any individual is to feel valued. How do your people know you value them? I once heard it said that people will not remember what you said and they will not remember what you did, but they will remember how you made them feel. Now there is something to think about! We will finish up with…

"**What do you need to do less of?**" Quit managing your people. They don't want to be managed. They want to be led. Stop telling them how to do their job and let them learn how to do it themselves. Better yet, educate them, empower them to a point where you don't even need to manage them anymore. Quit making their decisions. This is enabling, and as long as you take this approach they will remain dependent on you to do the thinking. Eventually, they will be afraid to make decisions and may stop thinking all together. The only way your people are going to become better thinkers is by learning how to think.

I will offer up one final thought on creating a strategy to develop your people. Competence leads to confidence, and if you don't believe in your people, at least believe they are capable of making quality decisions on their own, or they will never gain the confidence needed to perform at a high level. If you want your people to believe in themselves, you need to make sure they know you believe in them first.

Are you a BOSS or a LEADER?

A BOSS believes success is found in a great strategy. A LEADER knows success will be found in the people executing the plan.

A BOSS believes his or her employees are motivated by a paycheck. A LEADER knows their team is inspired by being part of a greater cause.

A BOSS believes they need to make decisions for their people. A LEADER believes in their followers to make their own decisions and empowers them to do so.

CHAPTER 15

———✤———

Stability Through Commitment

*"When you're surrounded by people who share a
passionate commitment around a common purpose,
anything is possible."*

~ Howard Schultz

I always encourage my clients to finish strong in
everything they do and I intend to do the same here. We
will wrap up our journey in the next chapter, discussing
some thoughts on trust. But equally important is the topic
of commitment. A business can withstand almost anything
as long as it has a core team of committed individuals. The
type of people I am referring to are those who will go the
extra mile when needed, those willing to make personal
sacrifices for the good of the whole. A business needs
leaders. I acknowledge there are committed bosses, but
only to a certain degree. When the going gets tough, they
get going—as in out the door.

Commitment is another one of those words thrown around, as if it happens by default. Don't fall prey to this misconception. Commitment is the product of being clear on both vision and purpose and believing in a greater mission than generating revenue. Commitment is the result of creating a culture that provides security, stability and a sense of pride in your product or service. Successful businesses are not only committed to the bottom line, they are committed to their communities, their shareholders, their customers but most importantly, to their people.

Some of the most productive discussions I have had with my clients relating to commitment start with this question: "What does commitment look like?" The answer is different in every organization because being committed comes from within. You can't learn to be committed. You can't train it and you certainly can't demand it. Commitment shows up in areas like engagement and passion. These are not taught and developed within the culture you create. I encourage you to ask your people or team this question. It won't take you very long to find out what is important to them. When you provide it, you will receive all the commitment you need.

If you want your people to be committed, you better be committed to them. If you really think about it, most relationships are built around the idea of reciprocity. It's a game of give and take. Generally speaking, if we give something we expect something in return. Commitment is no different. If I am going to be committed to you or to a business, it is natural to believe I will see some level of commitment come back. This may be oversimplified but it's the way we think.

I find it interesting how many issues stem from a lack of commitment or, more accurately, the fear of commitment. The most common fear of commitment is typically due to not knowing exactly to what we are committing. Understanding what is required within the commitment adds clarity, and clarity gives us comfort. *The fear doesn't come from what we know, it comes from what we don't know.* You expect your employees to be committed, but have you provided a clear picture of what that includes? Keep in mind that people want to be part of something. Commitment is something they desire but only under the right conditions. Confusion on what is required and what is expected is going to make the challenge of getting committed followers much more difficult. If you want followers, provide them a clear picture of what or to whom they are committing.

Another common issue with making commitments is that people lack an understanding of why they are making a commitment. What is the purpose that will be served?

What is the reason? It's no secret that commitment requires us to give a little more of what we have. It doesn't matter if it's time, money or some other resource, we need to clearly understand *why* we are making the commitment. The greater the understanding, the greater the level of commitment.

Once I introduce clarity and purpose into a conversation on commitment, my clients notice immediate and significant changes in both "committing to" and "committing from" in their respective businesses. When developing followers the same principles apply. Clarity and purpose make a major difference in the level of commitment your people will have both to the company and to you.

*****

This article offers 4 great points leaders must commit to.

4 COMMITMENTS
EVERY GREAT LEADER MAKES

What commitments are you making when you take on a leadership role? Your answer may determine how effective you really are.

"So much of success is a function of personal leadership," says Vince Molinaro, managing director for leadership solutions at Knightsbridge Human Capital Solutions and author of The Leadership Contract.

"I see the difference between those who show up every day very clear on what it means to be a leader, and others who are going through the motions," he says. "It's as if they clicked 'agree' on an online contract without reading the terms and conditions." By contrast, strong leaders know exactly what they're signing up for when they step into a leadership role.

It all comes down to these four commitments:

1. Leadership is a decision.

"You have to really define who you are as a leader, not just an individual contributor to the organization," Molinaro says. "Are you prepared to lead the way to whatever you believe is right? We've all worked with leaders who show up every day with that decision clearly made, and others who are just there."

One tell-tale sign is accountability. When things go wrong, do you blame external forces or others in your organization? Real leaders accept responsibility as the heads of their teams, and they're always working to do things better.

2. Leadership is an obligation.

Once you've made that deliberate decision to be a leader, you must accept that the expectations are higher for you than for everyone else in your organization. You have a duty to your team, your customers, and your community, Molinaro says. Part of that duty is holding to a higher standard of behavior than you might expect from those around you. Another part is recognizing your own limitations.

"For entrepreneurs and small business owners, the obligation may be to step outside your role," Molinaro says. "Some people are really good during the early growth phase of a company, but as it grows larger and needs to implement processes, that may not be their strength. Their obligation then may be to bring in a different leader for the next phase of growth."

3. Leadership is hard work.

"Leadership is hard, and getting harder," Molinaro says. "When you're running a business, there are a lot of great things that have to get done, and also some hard things." These might include repairing a client relationship that's soured, confronting an employee who isn't performing, or giving candid feedback to someone who needs it."

"It's human nature to avoid the hard stuff, but if you do, you weaken your company," he says. "If you have the courage to tackle the hard stuff, you become stronger."

4. Leadership takes a community.

This is an especially important commitment for small business owners, who often fall into feeling isolated in their positions. "You have to build a sense of community within your company, with bedrock relationships and people who can act as your advisors," he says. And you must nurture other leaders within your organization, and hold them to the same four commitments.

"When you do all that," Molinaro says, "customers can see the difference."[8]

*****

Now that we have identified how to get commitment, let's take a look at how to keep it. With every commitment there is also an expected outcome. It takes work to get commitment from your people. You can quickly lose them if they don't see the expected results from their investment. The clarity and purpose you provided in the beginning should have included a description of the expected outcome as well. This is a crucial element that, when overlooked, can result in a total disengagement of the person who originally made the commitment. Make sure you cover all the bases when you communicate those front end expectations.

Let's take a look at a much more important type of commitment—the commitment you will make to your people. Recall a couple of words you have seen already: stability and security. If you want loyal followers who are committed to you and your business, you are going to need to provide stability and security. These provide a controlled and safe environment. People follow those who make them feel safe. Bosses don't spend a lot of time thinking about safety, resulting in very few committed people.

There is one more aspect of commitment I want you to think about. A leader's commitment means staying consistent in what they say and do. Part of the commitment leaders exhibit is demonstrated by how and what they say when things don't go as planned. Commitment means you stay the course, and stay focused on the objectives set forth. Bosses will jump ship at the first sign of trouble, then justify their actions by making excuses for why they needed to head in a new direction. When making a commitment, we expect it to remain fairly consistent in words and actions along the way. A commitment to your followers is a commitment to the cause.

The difference between commitment or a lack thereof will make you or break you. Your people will quickly identify your failure to keep commitments. Your employees and followers will follow suit, and if the bar is not set high to begin with, it will be an uphill battle all the way.

The biggest mistake I have seen, related to commitment, usually occurs at the very beginning. Making decisions on what, or who, you are going to commit to is something that deserves a fair amount of consideration. The last thing you want is to be known as someone who doesn't follow through. Set yourself up for success, and make sure you know exactly what you are getting into before making a commitment, then follow through. For those who have made commitments to you, make sure you deliver on the expectations that were set forth at the beginning.

Here is a final thought on the value of commitment. Consider what is possible for those who are one hundred percent committed. Leaders create a culture in which following through on their commitment is the rule, not the exception. Things don't always go as planned, but staying true to your original commitments will establish credibility, and credibility produces trust.

Are you a BOSS or a LEADER?

A BOSS assumes commitment will happen by default. A LEADER knows commitment is the result of providing a very clear description of what is required, as well as the expected outcome.

A BOSS will tell employees to be committed. A LEADER will make ssure each individuals know why they should commit.

A BOSS stays committed as long as it serves their needs. A LEADER stays committed until the task is complete.

CHAPTER 16

———◆———

Trust Is About The Relationship

"Trust, not money,
is the true currency in business and life."

~ David Horsager

I've left this topic until last, because it is the most important one. Trust is the foundation of leadership and leadership is the foundation for follower-ship. You can apply any of the other thoughts and ideas I have shared earlier but the truth is without trust, you will not be able to develop followers, you will not be followed and you will never have a good reputation.

I want to break down this final chapter by looking at the progression of trust and how you gain or lose followers during the process. There isn't any part of your business that does not include trust. Trust is about relationships. Relationships built upon trust will always outperform those simply based on the numbers. I once had a client tell me he didn't need to trust someone as long as they were making him money. Are you kidding? Is this where you would want to invest your time or money, with someone you didn't trust?

The first challenge we have related to trust is building it in the first place. You have heard the saying that people do business with those they "know, like and trust." The know and like are pretty easy... but the trust element? That is an entirely different story. I can meet someone and like them after a twenty-minute conversation. Trust takes much longer to develop. To become trusted, you need a track record of delivering on your promises, putting others first and allowing others to grow in the process.

As individuals, we want to become more and to become more we must do more. If you want to do something you've never done before, you need to become someone you've never been before. Doing this is going to make you vulnerable, and there needs to be an element of trust that will provide both the security and confidence to do so. When you build trust with your people, they will be willing to take chances on becoming better because they know you have their backs. Even when an individual falls short, their leader will be there to support them. Bosses simply let him or her know, "It better be different next time."

Writing this book has brought back many memories both about the bosses and the leaders I have had in my life. I have reflected on how much trust I had for them and found there is a clear connection between the trust level I had and my willingness to follow them. Building trust is a common topic for discussion with many of my clients. You know I am a big fan of powerful questions. Another one of my favorites is, "Why should your people trust you?" I have had some very short discussions on this topic, which lets me know exactly where we need to start.

Building trust by definition is pretty straightforward. Do the right thing, deliver what you promised and be consistent in the way you do it no matter what. If you do this, your people will trust you. They will follow you. You may not remember back to when you were a follower but I can tell you your people are watching. They are watching for the person who is going to protect them, provide them opportunities and support them, even when they fall short.

Maintaining trust looks much like building trust. Remember the thought on "know, like and trust"? Well, now that you have followers, and they trust you, they are going to be looking to take the relationship to a deeper level. There are a number of ways you can maintain trust and, if done correctly, they will build a level of trust that will withstand the tough times you encounter. Make sure you continue to provide clarity on the vision and purpose of what you and your team are trying to accomplish. Know that your followers will struggle and fail along the way, and when they do provide compassion and encouragement to keep them focused in the right direction. *Remain strong in character.* We discussed earlier that most failures in leadership are the result of failures in character. There is no quicker way to lose trust than when you compromise your character.

Continue to build on your core competencies and those of your followers. Remember, they expect you to provide opportunities for growth and advancement. Stay committed to your word and your people. This maintains the desired stability and security. Stay connected to your people. As stated earlier, trust is about relationships and keeping your relationships strong will continue to build trust. Give your followers ownership in what they are doing. Your followers want to be part of the bigger picture; they want to make a contribution to the success of the organization. Remain consistent in everything you do and communicate regularly with your people. Let them know what is going on. *When your followers are given the opportunity to be part of the solution, they will be.*

Trust takes time to build and it is an ongoing process. The key is to make many more deposits than withdrawals at the trust bank. Something will eventually happen that requires you to make a significant withdrawal, and if you don't have enough in your account you may find you have lost the trust of your people from just one mistake. Don't find yourself believing you only need to have a certain amount of trust to keep people following you. The minute you stop investing in them and move your focus somewhere else, they will feel it and start looking in another direction for that safety and security we have been speaking about.

If something occurs that results in you losing the trust of your people, own it. The quickest way to restore trust is to be authentic and transparent and set a course for restoration. We all know not every decision made is the right one. It's up to the leader to make sure that when this occurs, all the facts are laid out on the table and the focus is on how to move forward. A colleague of mine puts it like this: "You need to let go of the past before you can embrace the future." Notice he didn't say "forget the past." We need to learn from every experience we go through, and trust will provide many lessons along the way. The information we learn from those lessons is not what will help us overcome them; the key is what we do with that information.

If there is one takeaway I would like to leave with you, it is the importance of trust; it is the lynchpin in a leader's life, and is the foundation on which all other topics we've discussed are built upon. You can go back through any of the chapters and see how trust plays a role. Don't get caught up in the idea that running a successful business is about the economy, the numbers, your competition, your product or your service. A successful business is about your people and the relationships you have with them. Their engagement, productivity, and their desire to play an active role in the organization will come down to the level of trust they have for their leader.

Here is my final thought about the value of forming strong relationships, founded on trust and secured by strong leadership: a boss puts most of their attention on the job and the service or product he provide. A leader will focus most of their attention on their people and followers. Leaders know success in business is really a bi-product of the people running it. So, what's it going to be? Are you a boss or a leader?

Are you a BOSS or a LEADER?

A BOSS's trust is implied because the employees have been hired to perform. A LEADER knows that trust is built over time and it has to be earned.

A BOSS focuses on creating a trusted product that meets specifications. A LEADER focuses on building trust with their people, who will own the outcome of what they produce.

A BOSS focuses on the job. A LEADER focuses on their people.

Chapter End Notes

1   http://goinswriter.com/perseverance-story/

2   http://ctb.ku.edu/en/table-of-contents/leadership/
leadership-functions/develop-and-communicate-
vision/main

3   http://www.forbes.com/sites/
erikaandersen/2013/08/29/3-simple-powerful-
things-leaders-can-do-to-inspire-people-to-do-great-
things/

4   http://www.entrepreneur.com/article/236591

5   http://www.inc.com/kevin-daum/7-ways-to-earn-
respect-as-a-leader.html

6   http://successnet.czcommunity.com/words-of-
wisdom/the-7-responsibilities-of-leadership/5528/

7   http://www.teamworkandleadership.com/2010/06/
leadership-accountability-that-may-move-you-to-
tears-true-story.html#sthash.Kh8JP0KY.dpbs_

[8] http://www.inc.com/minda-zetlin/4-commitments-every-great-leader-makes.html

ABOUT THE AUTHOR

Dave Ferguson is an internationally recognized executive coach, mentor, speaker, and trainer in the areas of leadership and personal development. Dave helps business owners, executives, top management leaders, and political leaders transform how they communicate, connect, and grow as leaders. He equips individuals, thought leaders, and organizations with high performance solutions to ensure continuous improvement in personal growth and business results.

Prior to starting his coaching company in 2007, Dave held several senior level leadership positions at mid-size and Fortune 100 and 500 corporations, where he successfully coached, mentored, trained, and developed leaders at every level. Dave has more than twenty years of experience in sales, leadership, business development, coaching and mentoring at both corporate and small business levels. He is a no-nonsense leader who has helped develop leaders at all levels.

Dave is also an Executive Leadership Coach for the John Maxwell Company, where he coaches executives internationally.

Dave resides in Davidson, NC and Hilton Head Island, SC.

Learn more about Dave at www.LivingtoLead.com